God's Purpose for the Family

God's Purpose for the Family

Stephen Kaung

Christian Fellowship Publishers, Inc.
New York

ISBN: 978-1-937713-38-6

Available from the Publishers at:

11515 Allecingie Parkway
Richmond, Virginia 23235
www.c-f-p.com

Printed in the United States of America

PREFACE

"And God created man in his image, in the image of God created he him; male and female created he them (Genesis 1:27). The concept of family had its origin with God at the very beginning when He created man, for God had an important purpose for the family to fulfill. Indeed, He will use *the* family of God—the church—to defeat His enemy, Satan. And hence, God's enemy is pouring out his fury to destroy the family.

Thank God, through the redemptive work of Christ, we Christians are to have our families restored to God's original purpose. This short series of messages, delivered by the author before a gathering of God's people in Washington DC beginning in September 1974, is therefore being published as a way of helping Christian believers elsewhere to see and carry out God's purpose for the family. May the Lord bless all who read the pages of this volume.

Contents

Unless otherwise indicated,
Scripture quotations are from the
New Translation by J. N. Darby.

Chapter One
The Origin of the Family

Genesis 1:26-28—And God said, Let us make man in our image, after our likeness; and let them have dominion over the fish of the sea, and over the fowl of the heavens, and over the cattle, and over the whole earth, and over every creeping thing that creepeth on the earth. And God created Man in his image, in the image of God created he him; male and female created he them.

And God blessed them; and God said to them, Be fruitful and multiply, and fill the earth, and subdue it; and have dominion over the fish of the sea, and over the fowl of the heavens, and over every animal that moveth on the earth.

Genesis 2:18-24—And Jehovah Elohim said, It is not good that Man should be alone; I will make him a helpmate, his like. And out of the ground Jehovah Elohim had formed every animal of the field and all fowl of the heavens, and brought them to Man, to see what he would call them; and whatever Man called each living soul, that was its name. And Man gave names to all cattle, and to the fowl of the heavens, and to every beast of the field; but as for Adam, he found no helpmate, his like. And Jehovah Elohim caused a deep sleep to fall upon Man; and he slept. And He took one of his ribs and closed up flesh in its stead. And Jehovah Elohim built the rib that he had taken from Man into a woman; and brought her to Man. And Man said, This time it is bone of my bones and flesh of my flesh: this shall be called Woman, because this was taken out of a man. Therefore shall a man leave his father and his mother, and cleave to his wife; and they shall become one flesh.

The notion of *family* is not something accidental; it is not something which originates from the will of the parents. Neither is it something initiated by the emotions of a man and a woman, nor is it governed by the customs of this world. To the contrary, *family* had its origin with God; that is to say, it is a divine concept. I think this is most vital to know and understand. We naturally view *family* as something human, and it is. And because it *is* human, we are inclined to view it as that which comes purely from the thought and idea of man. But the Bible informs us very clearly that *family* is God's idea; it is not man's. At the very beginning when God created man, He already had that concept in himself.

The Principle of Corporateness

The Bible says that God created man in His image. Now, what is the image of God? Of course, it is impossible for us to comprehend the total image of God, but one facet of His image which we do know is that our God is trinitarian in nature. Yes, there is only one God; nevertheless, at the time of Creation, this one God had said: "Let us make man in *our* image." And thus we find throughout the Scriptures the understanding that the

Godhead is composed of the Father, the Son, and the Holy Spirit. Such divine truth is a mystery to us, for it is impossible for us human beings to fathom the notion that our God, though being three in one, is nonetheless but one. On the one hand, we find that there is a plurality in God; on the other hand, there is a unity in Him.

In other words, one facet, feature or principle of the Godhead's image is that of corporateness—not individualism, but corporateness. And because God is such a God, when He said, "Let us make man in our image," the image of the man that He made is likewise corporate in nature: in His own image God created man as male and female. So we see that in the very creation of man the principle of corporateness is already there: neither the male is complete by himself nor is the female complete by herself. In the mind and will of God, the man of His creation is the union of a male and a female. And that, in brief, is the concept or notion of *family*. The family is built on the principle of corporateness.

The Family Not Nullified by Sin

We must always remember that *family* is God's idea, that it originated with Him. At the very beginning, when God created man, the family was already present. Yet for many today, the family seems to be a big problem.

Even at the time of Christ it was a problem. We will recall that one day some Pharisees came to Jesus and said, "Is it lawful for a man to divorce his wife for any reason?" And the Lord replied: "In the beginning God created male and female and joined them together as one. What God has therefore joined together, let not man separate" (see Matthew 19:3-6).

However, these Pharisees countered by saying, "Why is it, then, that Moses commanded that if a man gives a letter of divorce to his wife, he can divorce her?" But the Lord answered with these words: "It is because of the hardness of your heart that Moses allowed you to divorce your wives. Yet at the beginning it was not so. I say to you, therefore, that anyone who divorces his wife, except by reason of fornication, and marries another woman, commits adultery; and anyone who marries a divorced woman commits adultery" (see vv. 7-9). When not the Pharisees but the disciples heard *that*, they said to the Lord, "Now, if the relationship between a man and a woman is such as that, then it is better not to marry at all" (see v. 10). So even at the time of Christ, the institution of the family had become a serious problem for man.

Now some people have gone further to comment as follows: "Does not Paul say in I Corinthians 7 that he wished everybody would be like him and remain single? For Paul had written that if you are not yet married, if you are a virgin, or if you are a widow, then it is much better to remain as such because the days are difficult with many hardships, the time has been shortened, and the present form of this world is passing away." He had gone on to write: "I say this, not to control you, but to spare you" (see vv. 7a, 26, 29a, 31b, 35a, b). So people have concluded by observing that "if that be the case, and in view of the difficulties of our own time and of the soon coming again of the Lord Jesus, would it not be better that people remain single and not get married?"

Let me explain here that there *are* exceptions, and exceptions, as we often say, prove the rule. When Jesus' disciples complained about this issue of marriage vs. celibacy, He had explained that the latter is a gift, adding that whoever is granted that gift can remain single, but that it is not a gift granted to everybody. Some people, Jesus went on to say, are born eunuchs, others are made eunuchs by man, and some make themselves eunuchs for the sake of the kingdom of God; but to whomever this gift is granted, it belongs to them (see again Matthew 19, but now vv. 10-12). So I would stress the fact that throughout that same I Corinthians chapter, Paul does not nullify marriage or family life: he is only pointing out the exceptions.

I would reiterate that marriage and family originated with God and that the reality of family was already there at man's creation before sin ever entered this world. After sin's entrance, however, marriage and family have over time become such a problem that frequently people have concluded that it is better not to enter into marriage and that, furthermore, God's word grants that there are exceptions. But always bear in mind one important fact:

sin has not, and never will, nullify the notion of family which God had conceived in His mind well before sin entered this world. And thank God, through the redemption of the Lord Jesus He is able to restore not only individuals but also one's family to His original thought.

On the basis of God's word we need to firmly believe that the family has its origin with God and that though sin seems, to a certain extent, to have spoiled this divinely-ordained institution in the world, the redemption of the Lord Jesus is able to restore the family to the original thought of God.

God's Purpose for the Family

When God created man, why did He create a corporate man—that is to say, a family? Why did God create a union of two persons? It is because man was not only created in God's image, he was also created for a special work. God has a special task for man to fulfill. After God had created man, He blessed him and said, "Be fruitful and multiply, and fill the earth." How, though, can a single individual be fruitful and multiply and fill the earth? Impossible! And hence, it takes a family—a union of male and female—to do that.

Adam and his wife were not only to fill the earth by means of their multiplied offspring but the Bible says they were also to subdue it. Why was this further task commanded? Because they were to bring the whole earth—it having been repaired and made habitable once again by God following the devil's adversarial work of having earlier plunged the earth into darkness, emptiness and desolation (Genesis 1:1-2, 3, 6, 9-10, 14-15, 20-22, 24)—completely back to God that He might be glorified in all the earth. This was a tremendous task committed to that original corporate man whom God had created. Such a task can never be achieved by one individual alone; it must be done corporately; it has to be accomplished by the family. Therefore, as the original family multiplies into many families, and as over time the huge family of God—the church—comes into view, then through the church the earth is to be subdued; in other words, the kingdom of God is at last to be brought upon this earth.

God's Unit of Operation

The family is the unit of God's operation. We often incorrectly think of the *individual* as the unit of God's operation. But if we see that the man whom God created was a corporate man, then we must conclude that actually the family is the unit of God's operation and work. If God could have a family, and families, and *the* family, His work could be accomplished upon this earth. That is why God's adversary, Satan, is trying his very best to destroy the family; not only to destroy individuals but also to destroy the family. But thank God, the redemptive work of the Lord Jesus is not only for redeeming individuals but also families.

When God created Adam, He used the red earth and formed the body of the man. Then He breathed the breath of life into the nostrils of that body, and man became a living soul. Here thus was Adam. But after Adam had been created, God declared: "It is not good for man to be alone." Why so? Because God's concept was always the family. For one individual man could never do the work which God wills to give to man to fulfill. Hence God declared that it was not good for man to be by himself.

We frequently think that God had said it is not good for man to be alone because Adam was very lonely. Yes, he *was* lonely. But there was something more which lay behind God's declaration than merely Adam's loneliness. His solitary state did not fit in with God's concept; it could not fulfill His purpose. So God said, "I will make Adam a helpmate, his like." In other words, said God, "I will make for him a counterpart. He is just a part. So I will make him a counterpart and fit the two parts together and make man complete. This counterpart of My making will be Adam's likeness, just as he is. And this counterpart will be there to help him. By the cooperation and partnership of these two, My work shall be done." So because of that, God put Adam to sleep. God opened his side and took out something—perhaps a rib, say many Bible commentators—and God built a woman with that something. Woman was built from man, thus constituting Eve with the same material.

God Is the Matchmaker

Now the Bible tells us that God *brought* the woman He had made to Adam. It can be asked, then, who was the matchmaker here? According to old Chinese custom, in the olden days marriage was all arranged by the will of the two sets of parents and the word and counsel of a matchmaker. The man and the woman to be married never saw each other prior to their marriage. My father, when he was married, had never before seen my mother. It was his parents' will and the word of the agreed-upon matchmaker. My father was educated, and because of that, he was somewhat uneasy about this ancient arrangement. He did not know the woman he was to marry, and he could not even see that woman in advance. It was against the centuries-old custom. So, finally, he asked the help of a missionary lady to go visit that woman's family and try to see the woman for him. My father never saw my mother for the very first time until the day they were married. That was the way marriage came about in the olden days of my country.

Today in much of China and here in America it is not a matter of the will of the parents or the word of a matchmaker which brings two people together in marriage. Young people these days do not need any matchmaker because they match themselves. They try and try with all their cleverness and effort to find each other by all sorts of means. It is accomplished all on their own. But God's word tells us that in the matter of marriage it is neither the will of the parents nor the will of the man and woman; it is God who is the matchmaker. Adam did not go around trying to find a woman. God himself brought the woman to the man.

We Should Seek the Lord about Marriage

Some young people, who are not yet married, have talked with me about marriage. Sometimes I will ask: "Have you prayed about it?" Many young people who really love the Lord, who know they have to pray and seek the will of God in their lives about study and about this, that and the other, are, strangely, very hesitant to pray to the Lord about their mates. I have frequently asked this and that young brother or young sister, "Have you ever prayed about it?" Never, is their united response. It seems to be something embarrassing, even shameful. It seems marriage is something a person has to do himself or herself. People, it would appear, balk at asking God about it.

Yet let us acknowledge that marriage is one of the greatest events in one's life. It is a lifetime matter. Why, then, do you never really seek the Lord about it? In other matters you have no hesitation in asking and seeking the

Lord. Why is it that in the vital area of marriage, you undertake the task by yourself and fail to seek the Lord's face at all? Instead of running around, you should sincerely make it a subject of prayer. You should go before the Lord and tell Him that if it is His will that you should be married, then He should bring that mate to you just as He did in bringing Eve to Adam. Commit it to the Father; seek His mind and will about it. And if you do, He will bring her or him to you.

Weigh Everything Carefully before the Lord

Now when God said, "It is not good for man to be alone, I will make him a helpmate, his like," did He instantly proceed to make the helpmate? No. After God said, "I will make him a helpmate, his like," immediately God brought all the created animals to Adam. He brought all the fowls of heaven, all the beasts of the field, all the living things to Adam and let him name them. Now, why did God do that immediately after He said, "I will make him his counterpart"? For God certainly knew there was no such counterpart. God knew that among these beings there was no mate for Adam; and yet, before He proceeded to make that helpmate, He brought all these living creatures to Adam. Why? I think God was here giving man sufficient opportunities to choose. Though God is the One who, if asked to do so, actually matchmakes the marriage, He does it in such a gracious way. He will not force a person into doing something. God never does that. If allowed by man to do so, He will provide a person with plenty of opportunities to make one's choice.

If you commit your marriage to God, you will find that He will sovereignly raise up all kinds of opportunities for you to exercise your judgment. It was not a time for Adam to be emotional, that when he saw a monkey, he would be moved to declare: "That's almost like me. That is good enough." Had that been the case he would have missed the whole will of God. Adam was looking at all these animals with a longing for a mate, but he could not find his counterpart, his likeness. When Adam saw all these animals parading by, he had to be before the Lord about each one. He had to exercise a very cold mind and not be emotionally influenced or motivated. He carefully looked at every animal and gave each one a name, and, as it happened, each name perfectly fit. Every animal had its place, but he could not find his helpmate among them all. There was no registration within him regarding a counterpart for himself. He was looking for a counterpart, but because there was none, there was no suitable helpmate.

Sometimes young people are too impulsive and impatient; they rush into the task of selecting a mate. They too often quickly conclude, "Well, that's good enough." They cannot wait. Do not be in such a hurry. You have to weigh everything carefully before the Lord.

Though it may have seemed hopeless to Adam after all the animals had passed by with no helpmate having been found, he did not give up hope. God made an Eve for Adam. We, too, should not give up hope.

Hence, especially regarding this matter of mating, the Bible does show us that you should really be before God about it. You should truly commit this undertaking to Him and seek His will. Often, it is your own self that confuses everything. But if you truly seek your heavenly Father, He will provide opportunities for you to exercise your judgment. And, when the right person appears, there will be registration. For when Adam saw Eve, he declared: "This is it. This is bone of my bones and flesh of my flesh. This is woman." And the two were joined together in one. When God puts two people together as a family, then through that family His great work can be done. The family originates with God, and it is for doing His work and all for His glory.

Our heavenly Father, how we praise and thank Thee because the family is Thy *concept. How we praise and thank Thee that it is honorable and glorious. How we praise and thank Thee, sin cannot nullify the family because Thy redemptive work has restored it to Thy glory, and for this we praise and thank Thee. We now ask Thee to remember our Christian brothers and sisters who will be entering into family life; we pray that Thy glory will rest upon those families to be established, that together they shall truly serve Thee and serve Thy purpose. And, Lord Jesus, we especially commit the family of God—the house of God, the church of God—into Thy hands. We pray that Thou the Head of the house may bless God's house and bring it into such a favorable state that it shall be a true testimony to Thy name. We ask all in Thy name. Amen.*

Chapter Two
The Fall of the Family

Genesis 2:25-3:19—And they were both naked, Man and his wife, and were not ashamed.

And the serpent was more crafty than any animal of the field which Jehovah Elohim had made. And it said to the woman, Is it even so, that God has said, Ye shall not eat of every tree of the garden? And the woman said to the serpent, We may eat of the fruit of the trees of the garden; but of the fruit of the tree that is in the midst of the garden, God has said, Ye shall not eat of it, and ye shall not touch it, lest ye die. And the serpent said to the woman, Ye will not certainly die; but God knows that in the day ye eat of it, your eyes will be opened, and ye will be as God, knowing good and evil. And the woman saw that the tree was good for food, and that it was a pleasure for the eyes, and the tree was to be desired to give intelligence; and she took of its fruit, and ate, and gave also to her husband with her, and he ate. And the eyes of them both were opened, and they knew that they were naked. And they sewed fig-leaves together, and made themselves aprons.

And they heard the voice of Jehovah Elohim, walking in the garden in the cool of the day. And Man and his wife hid themselves from the presence of Jehovah Elohim, in the midst of the trees of the garden. And Jehovah Elohim called to Man, and said to him, Where art thou? And he said, I heard thy voice in the garden, and I feared, because I am naked; and I hid myself. And he said, Who told thee that thou art naked? Hast thou eaten of the tree of which I commanded thee not to eat? And Man said, The woman, whom thou hast given to be with me, she gave me of the tree, and I ate. And Jehovah Elohim said to the woman, What is this thou hast done? And the woman said, The serpent deceived me, and I ate. And Jehovah Elohim said to the serpent, Because thou hast done this, be thou cursed above all cattle, and above every beast of the field. On thy belly shalt thou go, and eat dust all the days of thy life. And I will put enmity between thee and the woman, and between thy seed and her seed; he shall crush thy head, and thou shalt crush his heel. To the woman he said, I will greatly increase thy travail and thy pregnancy; with pain thou shalt bear children; and to thy husband shall be thy desire, and he shall rule over thee. And to Adam he said, Because thou hast hearkened to the voice of thy wife, and eaten of the tree of which I commanded thee saying, Thou shalt not eat of it: cursed be the ground on thy account; with toil shalt thou eat of it all the days of thy life; and thorns and thistles shall it yield thee; and thou shalt eat the herb of the field. In the sweat of thy face shalt thou eat bread, until thou return to the ground: for out of it wast thou taken. For dust thou art; and unto dust shalt thou return.

After God created Adam with the dust of the earth and breathed into his nostrils the breath of life, man became a living soul. But God said, "It is not good for him to be alone." So He made him a helpmate, his counterpart. God took something out of Adam's body and with that He built the woman. He brought the woman to the man and immediately man said, "This is bone of my bones, and flesh of my flesh. She shall be called a woman, because she came out of man." And the two were joined together into one (see again Genesis 2:18-24). They were together in the Garden of Eden; and in the original language the word Eden means "pleasure." They were together enjoying one another and enjoying the Lord.

The Bible tells us that in the Garden of Eden these two were naked but they were not ashamed (see again Genesis 2:25). We will notice that all the living creatures which God had made were clothed with either feathers or fur. How is it, though, that when God created man, He did not clothe him with any kind of covering? Various Bible commentators believe that at the beginning man was clothed with glory and not with fur or feathers or some other covering; and that because Adam and Eve were clothed with glory they were not conscious of their nakedness. But, of course, after they had sinned, that glory departed from them and they became conscious of their nakedness.

Here we are told that before they had sinned the man and the woman were naked and yet they were not ashamed. I believe there must also be a spiritual significance behind this statement. They were naked; nevertheless, they were not embarrassed. What is the explanation? It is because their relationship with one another was so open and free of any reason for having guilt that there was bound to be a totally transparent relationship between the man and his wife. They were so one with each other that there was nothing to hide. Therefore, though they were without any covering, they were not embarrassed or ashamed. Such was the relationship between the man and the woman whom God had created. Adam and Eve loved each other. At this time they were of one mind, one heart, one spirit, and they were together serving the Lord. They had nothing to hide from each other. Indeed, we could say that their relationship was perfect; it was truly open and transparent. And this was not only so between the two of them, it was likewise true between them and God; for the Genesis account points out how God came down to the Edenic garden to fellowship with them.

The Essential Components of a Family

Now we human beings often think the essential components of a family are a man and his wife. Undeniably these two make up the family, but we may too easily forget that the family has another and very vital component. That important, even indispensable, component of a family is God. Our tendency too often is to think that a family is made up of a man and his wife and that if only they love each other, the family will be very happy and successful. But according to the word of God a family has another person present: even God himself. God had come into the Edenic garden to fellowship with Adam and Eve. He was not only the Creator of that family, He was one of the members of it. Not only was He one of the members, He was also the Lord of that family. Indeed, they would look up to God, they together would wait upon Him and allow Him to tell them what they should do! Their life together was one under God. There was perfect harmony between Adam and Eve on the one hand and between them and Him on the other. In short, it was a family under God. And that was God's original concept of what a family was to be.

The reason the family has become such a problem today is because man overlooks God as being one of the family. And when anyone leaves God out of the picture, things in the family begin to disintegrate. Even if there is a family on earth in which the husband and the wife love each other, and they seem to be very happy together, can it be said that that family is a success? From the human perspective it *is* a successful family, but from God's perspective it has not arrived at the meaning of what a family is to be as He views it. God is and should be part of every family, for He is the Head and Lord of that family. And because prior to sin Adam and Eve as a family looked up to God, therefore, they could live together in peace and harmony.

The Fall

As we have seen, before sin entered this world the first family on earth was a happy one, a family according to God's own thought. But then, something terrible happened. One day Eve was alone. She had drifted away from her husband, and when she was alone, the serpent—Satan, the devil—came forward to tempt her. The Garden of Eden was not at all small in size. For according to the description given in Genesis 2, we can accurately conclude that Eden's garden was a huge place. Nevertheless, heretofore Adam and Eve had always been together: they worked together, walked in the garden together; in fact, they were together in every activity. And hence, when they were together, God's and man's enemy had no opportunity to come in and to tempt. So the enemy was biding his time, waiting for an occasion when that family's members would be separated. Adam and Eve were always supposed to be together doing the Lord's work, and yet now they were found separated. When on this current occasion Eve was away from Adam and Adam was away from Eve, the opportunity for the tempter had finally arrived. We could rightly say here that Eve had begun to take an independent course. The family divided gives the enemy an opportunity to attack. When anyone in the family begins to take independent action—the husband going his way or the wife going her way, not being rightly related as partners of the grace of God—the enemy obtains an opportunity to come in, divide, and rule. That is the tactic of mankind's enemy.

In Ecclesiastes 4 Solomon tells us: "Two are better than one; because they have a good reward for their labour" (v. 9). Two are better than one. Not only will these two produce more by working together, but also, as they enjoy the fruit of their labor together, they will enjoy it better. In this regard, there is a difference between eating alone and eating together. Even if the same food is going to be eaten, if, instead of eating alone, you share and eat it with others, the food seems to have a better taste! It is much better for two to labor together and to enjoy together the reward of their labor.

Moreover, Solomon went on to say that "if they [both] fall, the one will lift up his fellow; but woe to him that is alone when he falleth, and who hath not another to lift him up!" (v. 10) It is very human for a person to fall, but if there be two of you together, then, should one slip, the other will lift him or her up. But if you are alone and fall, you will woefully fall flat.

Solomon in his wisdom was not yet finished. Said he further: "Again, if two lie together, then they have warmth; but how can one alone be warm?" (v. 11) You both engage in mutual support and aid, and by so doing each of you receives the warmth from the other. Finally, observed Solomon, "if a man overpower the one, the two shall withstand him; and a threefold cord is not quickly broken" (v. 12). The enemy can attack one solitary person, but two together can withstand his attack.

Because it is God who created the family, it is His desire that the husband and wife should be one in mind and spirit, that they be together and be rightly related one to the other under Him himself. And whenever this is the case, no one can stand against that family or its members.

For some reason, however, Eve was away from Adam. I wonder if her separation from her husband had occurred out of an intense curiosity regarding the forbidden tree. I do not know for certain if a woman is naturally more curious than is a man. Probably it is true. A woman's make-up, we know, is marked by a more emotional temperament, and thus, being more emotional, perhaps she is more curious. Generally speaking, man's temperament is more mental in character; therefore, he is cold and logical and not that curious. Eve, of course, knew that God had said that "of all the trees in the garden you may freely eat, but of the Tree of the Knowledge of Good and Evil, you shall not eat" (see Genesis 2:16-17a). Probably over time Eve had become quite curious about that tree. Nevertheless, I do not believe that in the beginning Eve had had any intention of eating that tree's fruit. That would be awful to think that she could rebel against God's command—and do it so readily and completely. No, such thought or intention had not come to her mind at all. She was simply curious: "Why is it that God does not allow us to eat of that tree? What kind of tree is this?" In the end, curiosity got the better of Eve, and hence, she just drifted away from her husband for the purpose of having a good look at that tree. But while she was thus alone and looking very closely at the tree, out of nowhere Satan appeared in the form of the serpent.

Now sometimes curiosity is good to have and to act upon it, but sometimes it can be very troublesome. If we are curious and it leads us to this or that forbidden area, then it can become *really* troublesome. So here was Eve, standing under this particular tree, intensely curious about it. And while she was thus engaged, the tempter came forth quietly, and softly, subtly inquired of her: "Did God say you cannot eat from any of these trees?"

Now, what did such inquiry signify? The man and the woman had been sustained in living by the fruit of the many trees in the Edenic garden, for that was part of their food supply ordained by their Creator—God himself. Yet Satan had clearly come forth to cast into Eve's mind an evil thought concerning what God had said. In brief, Satan's inquiry was meant to convey the idea that "God has a very hard heart; He does not want you to live." Eve said, "Oh, no. God said we may eat the fruit from any of the trees except from this one tree; He said we must not eat of it and we must not touch it, lest we die." She was now tempted, for God had only said, "You must not eat of this tree's fruit," but she had added to His word by saying, "You must not even touch its fruit." In other words, she was beginning to doubt God: "He is not that lovely a God after all, for has He not kept back something from us? He is not so good; in fact, He is being hard on us."

So Satan next comes forth to question God's word further by declaring to Eve: "No, you will not die; on the contrary, if you eat the fruit of that tree, your eyes will be opened and you will be as God." So Eve looked at the tree and its fruit even more closely than before. She now observed that it was good to look at, that it would give her wisdom to know good and evil, and that she would be as God. Instantly Eve forgot all about her Creator God; instead, she was now only thinking about herself—how to make herself God. It is clear that Eve had succumbed to the serpent's temptation, for she took hold of the forbidden tree's fruit and ate it. Not only did *she* eat it, she gave to her husband and he ate it also. Immediately they discovered they were naked; and they were embarrassed and ashamed, for they took some fig leaves and made aprons of them for covering themselves.

Separation of Husband and Wife

We often view the fall of man in terms of our *individual* ancestors who fell. In other words, how individual man fell into sin. But I would like for us to view the fall in terms of how mankind fell as a family. Let us see, first of all, that the fall actually began with the separation of the husband and the wife. It began with Eve taking an independent course, and hence, the two of them were now divided. That was the beginning of the fall of our ancestral family. When a family is divided in heart, when one member goes in one direction and the other goes in another—each taking his or her independent action—then that is the beginning of a family's fall. A family should be together under God; that is the protection and the glory of the believer's family. But when a family is divided by each going off along his or her own path, then that is the beginning of that family's fall.

Reversal of Divine Order

And second, let us see and understand that God had set a divine order in the original family. Adam, having been created first, was to be the head of that family. Only then was Eve created: she was built out of Adam and was thus to be the body of the family. Adam was set by God as the family's head, with Eve having been set by God as its body. The head without the body cannot do anything; and the body without the head has no sense of direction. So Adam and Eve—head and body—were together as the family. That was God's divine order. But in the course of the family's fall, that divine order was upset and reversed. For when Satan tempted Eve, she did not respond with the right attitude of: "Well, I will go back to Adam and consult with him and see what he says about this matter." Had she followed that attitude and action, she would not have been deceived. Eve, however, took the matter upon herself independently. More than that, she was the one in this family who took the initiative: she ate the fruit, and then gave some of it to her husband to eat. We see here that the divine order was reversed: instead of Adam being the head of that original family, he allowed Eve to be its head.

In the New Testament we are told by Paul in I Timothy 2 that it was not the man Adam who had been deceived but it was the woman Eve who had been and who had thus fallen into transgression (v. 14). However, in coming to Romans 5:12 we read that "by one man sin entered into the world," with that "one man" not being Eve but Adam. So far as the historical narrative of events is concerned, the woman was indeed the one deceived and who fell into transgression. But so far as God's interpretation or judgment is concerned, God held Adam responsible. Yes, Eve was the one deceived, not Adam. Adam ate the fruit with his eyes wide open. He knew it was a violation and a rebellion against the word of God. Adam well knew that, but he rebelled against God anyhow. Why? Because he loved Eve so much. He was willing to give up God but not give up the woman. Could we legitimately call that love? Actually, we shall find later on in the narrative that this was selfishness and not love on his part: in reality, Adam wanted Eve for himself, yet not out of love and concern for Eve, but out of concern for himself. Hence, when Adam sinned, he did so before God deliberately; and being the head of the family, God held him responsible.

Such is the sad story of the fall of the first family. There was manifested in this tragedy gross independence, and there was also a reversal of the divine order. It was these actions which brought in the fall of Adam and Eve and God's created family. And immediately after they together fell into sin the glory departed from them: these two now saw for the first time that they were naked and tried to cover themselves up.

Subsequently thereafter and in the cool of the day, God came down into the garden, but Adam and Eve hid themselves among the trees. Even their aprons of fig leaves could not hide their nakedness from God. So He called out: "Man, where are you?" And Adam replied, "We are here, hidden among the trees, because we are naked." But God inquired: "Who told you that you are naked? Have you eaten of that forbidden tree?" Instead of Adam standing forth and confessing by saying, "I am sorry; I did it," he lamely replied: "The woman that You gave to me, she gave the fruit to me and I ate it."

Can it at all be said that that was an expression of love? Being the head of the family, a man is supposed to protect, and even give his life—if necessary—for the woman he supposedly loves. But when it came down to a real life issue by God having begun to inquire as to what had happened, Adam simply declared, "It was the woman." Was that true love? Not at all. Adam's reply reflects the fact that when he ate the fruit, it was actually done so out of selfishness for himself and not for Eve's sake. He wanted Eve just for himself. Whenever sin enters a family's world, there is division and separation. Sin not only separates us family members from God, it also separates us family members from each other. Not only did the glory with which Adam and Eve had been clothed disappear, the love which had cemented them together also faded away. Instead of upholding that love, this first couple had become selfish, each of them trying to protect his self or her self; and love was now very much lacking in that first family.

God next asked the woman, "What is this you have done?" In response the woman placed the blame on the serpent: "It is the serpent that has deceived me." God proceeded, of course, to pronounce His judgment upon the serpent. After doing that, however, He turned His attention towards the family. Because of the family's fall due to the sin of rebellion which resulted in the loss of glory and the loss of love, that family was torn apart and God now began to pronounce His judgment upon each member of that family.

God's Unchanging Purpose

Yet even in His pronouncement of judgment upon the first family, God did not remove His original purpose from it. Thank God, He is a God of purpose, and when He purposes a purpose, He will never change it, no matter what happens. He may change His ways in relation to the accomplishment of His purpose, but He will never change the substance of His purpose. We shall indeed notice that His *ways* with Adam and Eve were going to be changed; nevertheless, even in His judgment upon this first family, God's *purpose* was not in the least changed. How do we know that? The answer is reflected in the words God now used in speaking to the woman: "Because you have sinned, therefore, with pain you shall bear children. You shall have pain in travail and in pregnancy."

When God had first created man and woman, He had said to them: "Be fruitful and multiply, and fill the earth." This command to be fruitful and multiply and fill the earth is, naturally, the work of the husband and the wife. Yet, it is the woman who bears the key responsibility here. She is to conceive, she is to travail, and she is to give birth to a child. That is the work which God had originally given to the woman to fulfill, and in fulfilling it, she would accomplish the work and purpose of God. And in pronouncing His judgment upon the woman for her sin God did not take that original purpose away; for He did not say to her, "From now on, you shall be barren. You will not serve My purpose for you anymore." Not so. The woman was still to conceive, to become fully pregnant, to travail, and to give birth. In other words, she is still to fulfill the original purpose which God had placed upon the woman of giving birth; but it will now be accompanied with *pain*. If, in the Garden of Eden, mankind had not sinned, there would have occurred many births, yet without any pain. But because the woman was deceived and followed an independent, rebellious course, God henceforth placed pain upon this woman and all other women thereafter whenever she and they experienced pregnancy and travail in childbirth. In short, God's ways had changed but not His purpose.

God further said in His judgment upon the woman, "You will desire after your husband, and he will rule over you." Why was He moved to state this? It is because the divine order, as God had first established between the man and the woman, had been overturned and reversed by what had occurred in the family's fall. But God now comes in in very clear words: that divine order is still to be maintained. In other words, even after the fall, God renewed in the woman a desire for her husband, and if she desires after her husband, she will give him the opportunity to rule over her as head.

From the very beginning the divine order between the husband and the wife had been there. Nothing about this had been mentioned specifically, yet it was obviously there. And prior to the fall of the family that order had been maintained out of love. Eve had had no need to be told to submit herself to her husband: she had done so out of love. But when love faded away due to the fall, God was moved to come forth and specifically declare the order, as though now putting the woman under a kind of obligation to desire after her husband, and he as head would rule over her. That divinely ordained order was still to be kept.

God's Judgment Is for Restoration

The third and final point which God had made clear in His judgment upon the woman was the fact that because the woman had been deceived by the serpent and had thus fallen into transgression, mankind's salvation shall come from the woman. Declared God in His judgment: "The seed of the woman shall crush the serpent's head, and the serpent shall bruise the heel of the woman's seed." We know from elsewhere in the Scriptures that the seed of the woman in view here is Christ Jesus. Out of the woman, and in the fullness of time, God sent His Son to be born of the woman under the law, so that He might deliver us out from under the curse of the law, and might bring us into sonship to God (Galatians 4:4-5). This tremendous promise was given to the woman, and it was to be fulfilled through the woman. Here we see that in judgment there is God's mercy. How gracious is our God! Even though He placed woman under His judgment, it nonetheless was not a hopeless situation. It was pronounced for the purpose of restoring her to the position where God had first placed her. Thus God's judgment here was not meant for destruction. It was meant for restoration, in order that the woman might be restored to the place which God had originally intended for her to occupy. Is that not beautiful?

Then God turned to the man in judgment. Because Adam had sinned, God declared: "The earth shall be cursed for your sake. With toil you shall eat your bread. The earth will grow thorns and thistles, and you will have to labor hard. In the sweat of your brow you can earn a living." Let us clearly understand that work in the Edenic garden before the fall had been pleasurable and not toilsome. Henceforth, however, God declared that the man's work will be toilsome: "You will have to sweat in order to earn a living." By these judgments pronounced upon Adam we see that God did not take away the duty of a husband. Rather, God now specifically placed the husband's duty upon him: you will have to work to support yourself and your family. Yet by doing that, the man may still be the head of the family.

We find, therefore, that in all of God's judgments upon both the man and the woman—upon both the husband and the wife—in God's original family, He did not set aside His original purpose. On the contrary, God was intent, through His judgments, to bring both the man and the woman back to the family which He had had in His mind even prior to His creation of the world and mankind. Hence, though His ways may change, His purpose always remains firm and unwavering.

So that when, in our future discussions together on the family, we come to the New Testament we shall see on the one hand that the man is to be restored to be the head of the family, that he is to provide for his family and bring up his children in the discipline and admonition of the Lord. And on the other hand, the woman is to be restored to her place in the family as a helpmate—as the one who is to support and build up the family. And thus family life is to be fully restored through the redemption of the Lord Jesus Christ.

Our heavenly Father, how we praise and thank Thee that Thou Thyself hast created the family and that Thou dost have a glorious purpose for it: that through the family the earth might be subdued and Thy kingdom may come upon this earth. Oh Lord, how we praise and thank Thee that Thou lovest us so much that even though our families have fallen, nevertheless, by Thy redemption Thou art going to restore them to their original glory. Oh, we just praise and thank Thee. May Thy words sink deeply *into our hearts and be very living and operative in us individually and in our families. We give Thee all the praise. In the name of our Lord Jesus. Amen.*

Chapter Three
The Salvation of the Family

Genesis 6:1—7:1—And it came to pass when mankind began to multiply on the earth, and daughters were born to them, that the sons of God saw the daughters of men that they were fair, and took themselves wives of all that they chose. And Jehovah said, My Spirit shall not always plead with Man; for he indeed is flesh; but his days shall be a hundred and twenty years. In those days were the giants on the earth, and also afterwards, when the sons of God had come in to the daughters of men, and they had borne children to them; these were the heroes, who of old were men of renown. And Jehovah saw that the wickedness of Man was great on the earth, and every imagination of the thoughts of his heart only evil continually. And Jehovah repented that he had made Man on the earth, and it grieved him in his heart. And Jehovah said, I will destroy Man, whom I have created, from the earth—from man to cattle, to creeping things, and to fowl of the heavens; for I repent that I have made them. But Noah found favour in the eyes of Jehovah.

This is the history of Noah. Noah was a just man, perfect amongst his generations: Noah walked with God. And Noah begot three sons, Shem, Ham, and Japheth. And the earth was corrupt before God, and the earth was full of violence. And God looked upon the earth, and behold, it was corrupt; for all flesh had corrupted its way on the earth.

And God said to Noah, The end of all flesh is come before me, for the earth is full of violence through them; and behold, I will destroy them with the earth. Make thyself an ark of gopher wood: with cells shalt thou make the ark; and pitch it inside and outside with pitch. And thus shalt thou make it: let the length of the ark be three hundred cubits, the breadth of it fifty cubits, and the height of it thirty cubits. A light shalt thou make to the ark; and to a cubit high shalt thou finish it above. And the door of the ark shalt thou set in its side: with a lower, second, and third story shalt thou make it. For I, behold, I bring a flood of waters on the earth, to destroy all flesh under the heavens in which is the breath of life: everything that is on the earth shall expire. But with thee will I establish my covenant; and thou shalt go into the ark, thou, and thy sons, and thy wife, and thy sons' wives with thee. And of every living thing of all flesh, two of every sort shalt thou bring into the ark, to keep them alive with thee: they shall be male and female. Of fowl after their kind, and of the cattle after their kind, of every creeping thing of the ground after its kind, two of each shall go in to thee, to keep them alive. And take thou of all food that is eaten, and gather it to thee, that it may be for food for thee, and for them. And Noah did it; according to all that God had commanded him, so did he.

And Jehovah said to Noah, Go into the ark, thou and all thy house; for thee have I seen righteous before me in this generation.

The Corruption of the Family

We have been considering together God's purpose for the family; and in the message for today I wish to continue somewhat with the history of the family as we find it recorded in a general way in the book of Genesis.

Now from our knowledge of that book we may recall that after the first family had fallen, Adam and Eve were driven out from the Garden of Eden. That first generation was certainly bad enough, but now let us look at the second generation. Adam and Eve had begun to have children—Cain and Abel. Both these children, once achieving manhood, came before Jehovah God to offer sacrifices. Cain offered up the produce of the ground that he had tilled, and he was rejected by God. By contrast, Abel offered up the firstling of his flock, and he was accepted by God. We know that God is not partial, but because Cain had offered up the fruit of his tilled ground instead of offering up the firstling of his flock, he was rejected. In his having done that, it showed that Cain did not believe he was a sinner needing the shedding of blood for the remission of his sin. On the contrary, he had thought he could go before God on the basis of his presumed personal righteousness and merits; indeed, on the basis of the work of his hands; so he offered up to God the produce of the ground he had tilled; but he was rejected. Abel, however, aware and acknowledging that he was a sinner, knew that he could not come before

Jehovah God except through the blood of a lamb. Accordingly, he offered up a more excellent sacrifice; and he was accepted by God. Abel was not any better than his brother, yet he offered up a better sacrifice. But when this entire event occurred, Cain, instead of being humbled by it before God, became jealous of his brother. So much so that one day, while both of them were talking out in the field, Cain rose up and murdered his brother (Genesis 4:1-8).

We earlier learned that during the first generation of the family sin had entered the world—more specifically, it had made entrance into the first family itself. And though that family had not been broken up by sin, love was nonetheless very much lacking already: the seed of failure and defeat of that first family had already been sown. And by the time of the family's second generation murder among the brethren had made its horrifying appearance.

Now when we come to the family's fifth generation, what do we find? There was a man named Lamech who ended up marrying two wives. As we well know, according to God's original design the family was to be composed of one male and one female, with the two of them becoming one flesh. Instead of observing and obeying that divine principle, Lamech proceeded to violate it and took two wives. Not only that, he had become a very vindictive person. For instance, he told his two wives that he had killed a young man because the latter had struck and injured him; so because of his hurt, Lamech had slain that young man. Moreover, he had gone on to declare to his wives that whereas if any man should kill Cain that person would be punished seven times, anyone touching *him* would receive in punishment seventy times seven (Genesis 4:15, 19-24). That was the sorry picture of what the fifth generation was like.

And when one reaches the *tenth* generation in this sordid history of the family, which happened to be the generation of Noah, there was not only the corruption of one family—and not only was there the corruption of the seed of Cain—but even the godly seed of Seth was also corrupted. In fact, by this tenth generation, the whole of mankind had become corrupted: all families upon the earth had become so except for one family—Noah's. Corruption had begun with the family, it then had spread to society, and finally it had spread throughout the whole inhabited world. We are told in the Bible that when the history of mankind had arrived at the tenth generation, God had looked down upon the earth and saw that it was full of violence, and that every imagination of the thought of man's heart was corrupt and continually evil. Think of that! Only ten generations had been necessary for the whole earth to have been corrupted. All the families had become so and man's imaginations were continually evil. There was not one good thought in man.

One contributing factor to the world's degradation at this time was the fact that during those days the sons of

God had observed that the daughters of men were most fair and beautiful. So these sons of God willfully took to wife the daughters of men as they chose. And out from such unions came forth giants, the so-called "heroes" and "men of renown." Why were they referred to in this way in Scripture? Because they were half man and half spirit. These sons of God were fallen angels. How do we know this? We learn from the book of Job—chronologically the first of all the Bible books to have been written—that the phrase "the sons of God" is a reference to angels (Job 1:6, 2:1). Hence, the Genesis narrative, written subsequent to Job, would not have needed to explain who these sons of God were, it being understood that angels are being referred to; and that these were *fallen* angels, since such created beings were never intended by God to either marry or be given in marriage. Therefore, these angels had willfully acted against their very nature. They had not kept their proper place as angels, just as the New Testament writer Jude has informed us (v. 6). In disobedience these fallen angels had come down to the earth and had intermingled with the daughters of men, and out of these forbidden unions had come forth hybrid beings. From the human perspective they were incredible giants; but from God's perspective they were the product of the violation of His established order. Because angels belong to one class of created beings and man belongs to another, the action of these angels constituted a gross violation of divine order.

God Repented of Making Man

When it came to the time of Noah, therefore, God saw that every family—indeed, the whole earth—was corrupt. And in righteous reaction God declared that He repented of having created mankind. It must have been a terrible thing for God to have had to say that He repented of having made man. Moreover, God also declared that He was going to destroy all living things upon the earth.

Was God in need of repentance here? God is not a person that He should repent. *We* need to repent—and often; but God is certainly not one who needs to repent. Why, then, does the Bible say that God repented of His making man? We need to be clear here that so far as God's *purpose* is concerned, He shall never repent: once He sets forth His purpose, He will unceasingly work in relation to that purpose until it is totally fulfilled. He never changes His purpose. He never does and never will. But with regard to His *ways*, God sometimes repents—that is to say, He will repent of or change His methods.

Let me employ an imperfect illustration here to demonstrate the point just now made: parents in relation to their children. You who are parents, what is your longing, purpose and aim for your children? You greatly desire your children to grow up to reach manhood and womanhood, to be mature men and women. Would you ever change that wish or desire? Certainly not. From the day a child is born until he or she becomes a man or a woman, you as parents never repent or change your heart desire and purpose regarding your children: you want them to grow up to manhood and womanhood. Even so, during the process of their growing up you will often change your way of dealing with them. For example, at first, when they are little babies, you deal with them in ways called for during babyhood; you love them, provide for them, and as soon as they cry, you give the bottle to them. How patient you are with your babies! But when the baby begins to grow out of his or her babyhood, then you not only continue to provide for them but you also begin to teach them and even discipline them, too. You do not exercise the latter too strongly because they are too young. Nevertheless, discipline begins. Then, when they grow up somewhat more, you must teach them and discipline them further. The way of discipline will continually undergo change as your children continue to mature.

And thus, you change your way of dealing with your children, but you never change your purpose and desire for them. With some children, if you beat them they are finished. With other children, if you do *not* beat them, they are finished as well. You have to be sensitive to the individual character of each child and treat each of them accordingly so that they may grow up to manhood and womanhood. If one method does not work, you will repent and change to another method but your purpose towards your children never changes.

Noah Found Favor in God's Sight

So is it with God who never needs to repent of His purpose; but with the coming in of righteous Noah's generation He is going to change His method towards mankind. God had declared He would destroy all mankind on the earth. But thank God, Noah found favor in His sight. Let us observe here that in comparison with his terribly wicked generation Noah stood out as most just and righteous. And consequently, he found favor in God's eyes; nevertheless, such favor bestowed upon Noah was all of grace.

Now before God carried out His intent to destroy the world, and because Noah had found favor in God's eyes, He told Noah to build an ark. It was not to be a simple little chest for preserving himself, though that is what an ark is actually for. No, the first ark ever built turned out to be a tremendous and quite substantial ship. We recall that much later the mother of Moses would place her son in a little chest. It was in reality an ark, and it was only good enough for preserving and sheltering a baby (Exodus 2:1-3). But here God had commanded Noah to build not a small chest or ark but a tremendous vessel. Why such a large ark? Because when God commanded Noah to build an ark, it had to be spacious enough to accommodate Noah, his family, and two each of all the living creatures. We understand, of course, that the ark—in Biblical type or symbol—is representative of Christ because of the sin of this world. We will recall the Lord Jesus saying: "As were the days of Noah, so shall it be at the coming of the Son of man" (see Matthew 24:37).

If we compare our time with that of Noah, we shall find numerous similarities. In our time the earth is full of violence. In addition, how the imaginations and the thoughts of man are continually evil as reported in the newspapers, on television, and on the radio! Moreover, we notice how in advertisements everywhere every thought and every imagination is continually evil in character and pollutes human minds. Let us also observe the condition of the families today. Families are disintegrating and breaking up, having been corrupted by the world. Then, too, spiritism is prevailing today, just as it was in the days of Noah. Because of all which had marked Noah's generation, God's judgment was to come upon the entire earth. And if that was true of Noah's day, can the earth today escape a similar judgment? Considering the situation in our day, surely God's judgment is not far hence in coming upon this world.

But thank God, He has provided an ark for us by which to escape that judgment, and our ark is, of course, the Lord Jesus. God has provided Him as an ark for man that whoever believes in Christ may escape judgment and be preserved in Him. And *this* ark of God's is immense; in other words, so far as the salvation of the Lord Jesus is concerned, it can contain and include every believer: it is not just for one person; His salvation can be for every member of every family in this world. Such is the immensity of the salvation of Jesus Christ.

Now Noah's ark was made of gopher wood, and we are told by Biblical scholars that gopher wood is considered to be incorruptible. This speaks of the humanity of the Lord Jesus. In order to save us He who is God had to become flesh—that is, He must take up the form and likeness of man; and yet, *His* humanity is perfect, is sinless—in this respect, His humanity is not like ours. Noah's ark was also covered within and without with a layer of pitch. This latter word in Hebrew is the same word translated as our English word *atonement*. This speaks of the Lord Jesus having come to earth as a man in order to atone for man's sins.

Of course, there was a door in the ark; which is to say that believing mankind can enter in. The door, however, was not only for making entrance; it was also for shutting out, for the preservation of those within. In other words, whoever enters by believing into Christ is saved, kept and preserved, so that when judgment shall come, that one shall be kept safe within.

The ark had not only a door, there was also a light up above. The original Hebrew text reads: *the* light. In some Bible versions the word light is translated as window; but actually it should be translated as the light. The picture for us here, therefore, is that in Christ we are divinely guided from above. Hence, from all these various descriptions of the ark given here, we can readily discern that Noah's ark speaks of Christ for us today.

So in the days of Noah God had commanded him to build an immense ark, He additionally noting that man's days hereafter shall be 120 years and no more once the flood arrives (see Genesis 6:3b). Noah believed God and began to construct the ark. Now we must remind ourselves that up to Noah's time there had never been any rain. The earth had simply been watered by means of the mist that periodically descended upon the ground (Genesis 2:4-6). Just think of that fact for a moment: there had never been any rain, and yet God had commanded Noah to build an ark! What faith upon Noah's part!—but also what mocking he had to endure! For the people of that day mocked and laughed at him unmercifully, saying continually to him: "Noah, something must be terribly wrong with you! From where will come the flood waters about which you so confidently preach to us daily?" No one had ever seen rain; and yet, by faith, Noah continually built the ark despite the mocking.

Noah's Family Was Saved

During all those 120 years which God had proclaimed, Noah remained a steadfast preacher of righteousness. He began to preach to all who came to him, but none believed him, not even one (II Peter 2:5, Matthew 24:38-39). But his wife believed him; his three sons believed him; and also his three daughters-in-law believed him. Though the rest of the world rejected his preaching, his entire family believed in what he believed.

How righteously Noah must have lived before his family! We would observe that people who do *not* know us can believe and have confidence in us somewhat easily, but for people with whom we live day and night to believe us, that must surely be very difficult for us to inspire such faith and confidence. Hence, what an exemplary life Noah must have therefore daily lived in the presence of his family! Only this could account for how it was that though the entire world did not believe him, his whole family ended up believing what he believed. There eventually came a day when God commanded: "Go into the ark, you, your wife, your sons, and your daughters-in-law." There were eight of them who did so. They all entered the ark and when the flood came, that entire family was saved.

We have noted before that the family of man had fallen terribly from God's original design. It had descended to the very bottom and had to be completely wiped out. But thank God, in the midst of such degradation and failure there is salvation; but please observe that when God provides salvation, it is for the family and not merely for one individual. In reading the relevant Bible text we shall notice that it declares that it was Noah who was righteous before God. It does not say that Noah, his wife, his sons, and his daughters-in-law were all righteous before Him but makes clear that it was

Noah who had been righteous before Him and that God thus remembered Noah and saved his entire family.

We therefore can see from this that it is the family which has fallen; and so, in the redemption of the Lord Jesus, God comes not only to redeem one or two individuals but comes to redeem the family as well. Thus, with regard to the unit of salvation, it is the family; but with respect to your receiving the Lord Jesus for salvation it is an individual matter. It is quite true that we each of us must believe in the Lord Jesus to be saved. Our parents cannot believe for us and neither can our children believe for us. Each person has to believe in the Lord Jesus to be saved. All that is very true. However, there is a further aspect to God's salvation in Christ which must be considered more closely according to the entire Scriptures.

God's Promise for the Family

Let us recall from Acts 16 what God's servants had said to the Philippian jailer when asked by the jailer what he must do to be saved. Declared Paul and Silas: "Believe in the Lord Jesus and you shalt be saved, *and* your household" (v. 31). That is God's original order on the matter. If you believe in the Lord Jesus, you shall be saved. Believing in the Lord Jesus is a must for a person to be saved. But God then promises: "... and your household." In other words, because God's salvation in Christ has been provided for the whole family, therefore, when one person in the family is saved, He promises to give that person His salvation to his entire family.

I want to emphasize the Biblical fact that the provision of the Lord's salvation is for the family. If you have believed in the Lord Jesus, God has a promise for you. He promises to give you your whole family. It is true, individually every member of your family has to believe in the Lord; nevertheless, they are promised to you who have already believed in Jesus for your own salvation.

All the promises of God are yea and amen in Christ Jesus (II Corinthians 1:20); even so, all the promises of God have to be accepted by faith. God makes many promises to us in His word, but these promises are not fulfilled automatically or mechanically. They must come about by a person's exercise of faith. Let me put it another way. Here is a promise of God. It cannot and will not be fulfilled mechanically or automatically. Someone has to claim that promise by faith: "Oh Lord, You have promised it, make good on that promise." And when that person lays claim to the promise by faith, God honors that promise and will act on it.

Some people have said the following: "I have believed in the Lord. Why is it, then, that my family is not saved? Why is it that my family does not come to the Lord?" It is because with God nothing comes forth mechanically: because He is a living God, everything must be living. Therefore, whenever God makes a promise to us in His word such as this one regarding family salvation, He waits for you to rise up in faith and claim it for His glory. And if you lay claim to this promise, God will fulfill it. Moreover, if you by faith have claimed this particular promise, you should live in obedience to Him so that you may be a light in your family. And, then, when those others in your family see the light, they will receive the Lord's salvation and give glory to God.

Hence, let us realize that, on the one hand, God does promise us in His word that if each of us believes in the Lord Jesus, our whole household shall be saved; but that, on the other hand, for that promise to be fulfilled, we each need first to claim it by faith, and second, each of us must live a life of obedience to the Lord in order to provide light in one's family. Only then will God's promise come upon our households. Even as God saved Noah and his family, so God can save us and our families.

Families Saved in Egypt

Now when we consider the time when the children of Israel came out of Egypt, the same salvation was true of their many families. The Israelites at that time were slaves in Egypt, and God used the first Passover event to save them from death and deliver them out of Egypt. God told the children of Israel that every family should prepare a lamb. It was not the case that each and every person should prepare a lamb but every family. On the fourteenth day of the Jewish calendar's first month every family was to kill a lamb and sprinkle its blood upon the doorposts and the lintels of the house. The whole family was to be gathered inside the house, and they were to roast the slain lamb and eat it in preparation for departure from Egypt.

Why the sprinkled blood? Because on that night wherever God, in passing through the whole land of Egypt, saw the sprinkled blood He passed over that family's house. If, though, there were no blood to be seen, then the angel of destruction would enter that house and kill that household's firstborn son. It was to be a slain lamb per family, but if a family were too small and were thus not able to eat the entire roasted lamb, that family was instructed to share with its neighbors (Exodus 12:1-13, 21-23, 28). In other words, a given family could be enlarged. Such a circumstance depended on one's faith: if the faith of the family head was large, more people would be included in that family. But if one's faith was small, it nonetheless resulted in at least one's immediate family having been saved that night in Egypt. Hence we see that in the case of that long ago Passover event, it was to be a lamb for each household.

Here again we observe a consistent pattern in the Bible regarding the matter under discussion: that God's salvation is meant for the family.

Rahab's Family

When the Israelites entered the Promised Land, the first city they were to take was Jericho. Two spies slipped into that city to spy on it. They entered the house of the harlot, Rahab, who had secretly welcomed them inside. But the king of Jericho heard rumors to this effect and sent his agents to Rahab to learn the truth. They inquired of her: "Did you see two men from the Israelites come your way?" Now Rahab was convinced that Jericho would be destroyed by God's people; she therefore had faith in the God of the Israelites. So instead of turning the two spies in, she hid them in her house. These two spies instructed and promised her just one thing: "You must gather together your family—your father, your mother, your brothers, your sisters, your relatives—in this house where you must outwardly display a scarlet thread. And when we come back with the others to take this city, all who are gathered and remain in this house shall be saved." The Bible tells us that Rahab indeed gathered her family—father, mother, brothers, sisters, and relatives—and they all stayed in the house during the Israelite assault on Jericho. And hence, because of the faith of Rahab, that entire household was saved (Joshua 2:1-21, 6:17, 22-23, 25; Hebrews 11:30-31).

Now if the head of a given family believes in the Lord Jesus, it will be much easier for the whole family to come to the Lord and the entire household to be saved. But this is not necessarily what happens in every case. For instance, Rahab was obviously not the head of her family, and yet she had faith and trusted in the Lord (Hebrews 11:31). So God promised through the two spies that the entire family of Rahab would be saved. And, of course, all her immediate family members and all her relatives had to believe *her* and remain in the house in order to be saved. Had they in unbelief wandered out onto the street, they would have been killed (Joshua 2:17-19). Thus we see that each of them had to believe for themselves.

The House of Cornelius

When we come to the New Testament once again, we learn that the same circumstance occurred in the house of the Roman centurion officer, Cornelius. He was thus a Gentile who nonetheless was a very godly person: he with all his household feared God, earnestly and constantly prayed to Him and generously gave alms to the Jewish poor. His prayers were ultimately answered, for one day an angel of God appeared to him, saying: "Send to Joppa and have the man called Peter to come, and he will tell you what you need to hear." So he sent his servant there; and when Peter came to Cornelius, he found that this Roman soldier had gathered together not only his immediate family and relatives but also his many friends. While Peter was yet speaking the gospel to the assembled household, the Holy Spirit came upon every one of them:

Cornelius, his family, his relatives, and even his intimate friends. From God's perspective, they were all included in the household of Cornelius. His faith had been great (Acts 10, esp. vv. 2, 22, 33, 43-44). Oh, may God also give us that kind of faith!

Lydia's Household

In coming to Acts 16 again, we read of Lydia's household. Lydia was a businesswoman handling purple fabrics. In fact, she was conducting a rather large business, because at that time anyone dealing with purple was deemed to be a prince among merchants. Even so, though Lydia carried on a prosperous enterprise, she nonetheless feared and worshiped God. In listening to Paul, she and her whole household believed the gospel and were baptized (vv. 13-15). This had occurred in the same city of Philippi where the jailer of Paul and Silas, together with his entire family, had likewise been saved. These two households in Philippi rejoiced greatly in the Lord.

Let us never lose sight of this one fact: God's original purpose is the family. Therefore, in the salvation which He has prepared for us, He not only has the individual but also the family in view. It is household salvation that God is ultimately after. Oh, may we rise up in faith and claim this promise before God! May we also live in obedience to God and thus serve as light to our families. If so, we shall witness family after family coming to the Lord.

Finally, let me inquire: Do we realize that the building block for the church is the family? If the family is strong before God, the church will be strong. If, though, the family is weak, the church shall also be weak. How necessary it is for all believers to see this truth. God is faithful with regard to family salvation. Let us therefore believe and claim His promises. Let us act on this truth by faith and live faithfully into it; and we will see that our families, our children, our grandchildren—generation after generation—will belong to the Lord, and as families will serve God together. May His name be glorified.

Our heavenly Father, how we praise and thank Thee for Thy provision. Thou dost provide Thy salvation for the family. It is Thy promise that if we believe on Thy Son, we each individually shall be saved, and also each of our households. Oh God, we do rise up in faith and claim this promise from Thee. And we ask Thee to be merciful to us, that we may all live as a light before our family members. And we do expect Thy promise to be fulfilled in each of the families represented here, and in the families of Thy people everywhere. We pray that Thy church will be built and that Thy name may be honored and glorified. We pray in the name of our Lord Jesus. Amen.

Chapter Four
Choosing a Mate

Genesis 24:1-27—And Abraham was old, and advanced in age; and Jehovah had blessed Abraham in all things. And Abraham said to his servant, the eldest of his house, who ruled over all that he had, Put thy hand, I pray thee, under my thigh, and I will make thee swear by Jehovah, the God of the heavens and the God of the earth, that thou take not a wife for my son of the daughters of the Canaanites, among whom I am dwelling; but thou shalt go to my land and to my kindred, and take a wife for my son Isaac. And the servant said to him, Perhaps the woman will not be willing to follow me to this land: must I, then, bring thy son again in any case to the land from which thou hast removed? And Abraham said to him, Beware that thou bring not my son thither again. Jehovah the God of the heavens, who took me out of my father's house, and out of the land of my nativity, and who has spoken to me, and who has sworn to me, saying, Unto thy seed will I give this land—he will send his angel before thee, that thou mayest take a wife for my son thence. And if the woman be not willing to follow thee, then thou shalt be quit of this my oath: only, bring not my son thither again. And the servant put his hand under the thigh of Abraham his master, and swore unto him concerning that matter.

And the servant took ten camels of the camels of his master, and departed; now all the treasure of his master was under his hand; and he arose and went to Aram-

naharaim, to the city of Nahor. And he made the camels kneel down outside the city by a well of water, at the time of the evening, when the women came out to draw water. And he said, Jehovah, God of my master Abraham, meet me, I pray thee, with thy blessing this day, and deal kindly with my master Abraham. Behold, I stand here by the well of water, and the daughters of the men of the city come out to draw water. And let it come to pass, that the maiden to whom I shall say, Let down thy pitcher, I pray thee, that I may drink, and who will say, Drink, and I will give thy camels drink also, be she whom thou hast appointed for thy servant Isaac; and hereby I shall know that thou hast dealt kindly with my master.

And it came to pass before he had ended speaking, that behold, Rebecca came out, who was born to Bethuel, son of Milcah the wife of Nahor, Abraham's brother; and she had her pitcher upon her shoulder. And the maiden was very fair in countenance; a virgin, and no man had known her. And she went down to the well, and filled her pitcher, and came up. And the servant ran to meet her, and said, Let me, I pray thee, sip a little water out of thy pitcher. And she said, Drink, my lord! And she hasted and let down her pitcher on her hand, and gave him to drink. And when she had given him enough to drink, she said, I will draw water for thy camels also, until they have drunk enough. And she hasted and emptied her pitcher into the trough, and ran again to the well to draw water; and she drew for all his camels. And the man was astonished at her, remaining silent, to know whether Jehovah had made his journey prosperous or not.

And it came to pass when the camels had drunk enough, that the man took a gold ring, of half a shekel weight, and two bracelets for her hands, ten shekels weight of gold, and said, Whose daughter art thou? Tell me, I pray thee. Is there room in thy father's house for us to lodge? And she said to him, I am the daughter of Bethuel the son of Milcah, whom she bore to Nahor. And she said to him, There is straw, and also much provender with us; also room to lodge.

And the man stooped, and bowed down before Jehovah, and said, Blessed be Jehovah, God of my master Abraham, who has not withdrawn his loving-kindness and his faithfulness from my master; I being in the way, Jehovah has led me to the house of my master's brethren.

Let us be reminded by way of a brief summary what has been covered thus far in our consideration together concerning this important subject of the family. At the very beginning of our discussion it was pointed out that the very idea of *family* is not a human but a divine concept. For when God had created man, He had done so in such a manner that when the creative process had been completed, what emerged was actually a family; that is to say, it was corporate in nature. Indeed, God created both a male and a female, and brought them together in order that the two might be joined into one flesh. So far as God's purpose in creation is concerned, family is definitely in God's will.

It was then noted that later on, in relation to the redemption and salvation of the Lord Jesus, God made it clear in His word that the family formed the basic unit for salvation. In the New Testament Book of Acts chapter 16, for example, we are first instructed that each of us must believe in the Lord Jesus personally and be saved (for, said Paul to the Philippian jailer, "Believe in the Lord Jesus and you shall be saved"); but we are then instructed in God's word that not only each of us who believes shall be saved but also our household or family (for Paul added: ". . . and your house"). In other words, the salvation of the Lord includes not only each one of us but also each of our households. All we who believe in Jesus can claim this promise from God. If each of us believes, and if each of us also lives obediently before the Lord, God will honor His promise and each and all of our families shall be saved.

We can therefore rightly conclude that because the family is of such importance, its formation and how one goes about it is a very serious matter. If we want to see God's purpose in the family totally fulfilled, and if we wish to see God's glory manifested in the family, then from the very outset in the formation of a family we as believers should be very careful before God. Therefore, I would like for us to consider together this matter of choosing a mate.

Obviously, what will be said here will be specifically directed towards those who have not yet formed families. If, by the sovereignty of God, you already have a family, please be reminded that you must not look back. You shall not decide, "Well, I'll try to begin all over again." No. If you already have a family, you can only look forward. In other words, whatever may be your current status, you must look to the Lord for His mercy and grace so that your family may be what He wants it to be. Hence, never look back; only look forward.

For those, however, who have not yet formed families, the word of God has definite instructions with regard to this endeavor of choosing one's life-companion. This undertaking is extremely important because it will not only affect the future of *your* family, it may very well affect the second generation and even other generations to follow. It very well may also affect the church, the general society, and even possibly the whole world; but even more so, it may affect the purpose and glory of God. So for the sake of the glory of God and His purpose, this issue of choosing a mate is of tremendous significance. We who are the Lord's therefore need to look to God in this entire endeavor and be guided continually by His word.

Now there is a most beautiful story in the Bible related to this very subject of choosing a life-companion. I would like to utilize this story—found in Genesis 24—as an apt illustration and try to draw out from that story some of the guiding principles for choosing a mate.

Marriage Originates with God

Abraham was well-advanced in age, so he summoned his steward, Eliezer (Genesis 15:2), the eldest of his servants, and said, "Go back to the land where I came from and secure a wife for my son Isaac." Let us first notice that it was Abraham who launched this entire undertaking. In the context from God's word now before us we can say that Abraham represents God himself. And we know from the opening chapters of Genesis that God is the Originator of marriage and of the family. At the Creation when he created man, He had declared: "It is not good for man to be alone. I will make him a helpmate, a counterpart." Yet not only that, even as regards this subject currently before us of mating—which is to say, the bringing of two people together—we see from God's word concerning Abraham that it begins with God.

God Creates the Need and Provides the Supply

Physically and psychologically there comes a point in a person's life when he or she begins to feel the need to have a mate, a life-companion—if you will, a family. Now when that need begins to be felt in a young brother or a young sister in the Lord, what should he or she do? Too often such Christian brethren conclude as follows: "Here is a human need of mine. Because I have such a need, I must therefore go out and find the supply to that need." As Christian brothers and sisters, however, what should be the proper reaction for you to follow when you begin sensing the need for a life-companion? Let us all realize one important fact here: that even this particular need which you are currently feeling comes from God. He has created you in such a way that He has placed in you such need and its sensing. There is therefore nothing wrong with the desire you sense to have a life-companion and enter into a family relationship. It is clearly of God himself. And hence, when you begin to sense that desire, the first reaction on your part is not to go around attempting to obtain the supply yourself. Rather, your first reaction as a Christian is to go to God and pray: "O God, You have put that need and desire within me; so now You will have to provide that needful supply. You yourself will have to find the right mate for me. I am looking to You to choose that mate for me."

Yes, in one sense we do choose our mates, but in another sense we do not: ultimately, it should be God who chooses our life-companions. Therefore, whenever you begin to sense the need to have a life-companion, the first principle to observe in this endeavor of choosing a mate is for you to bring the matter to God. Let us not be so conservative in thinking that it is embarrassing to bring such a need before Him. As believers in Christ, are we not instructed in God's word to bring every concern, every problem and every need to God? (I Peter 5:6-7) And from among all our needs, this particular one is a lifetime one, indeed. And hence, because it is such a vital issue, how can we feel in the least reluctant to go to our heavenly Father and tell Him of our need and ask Him to supply it?

Most certainly this is what every believing brother and every believing sister should do.

"Go to My Homeland"

Abraham called his steward and made him take an oath, saying, "Do not secure a wife for my son from the women of the Canaanites where I am now dwelling. Go to my homeland and obtain a wife for my son from my kindred." The servant said, "Suppose the woman is not willing to come here. Should I take your son to the land you came out from?" Abraham replied: "No. God has brought me out and has promised to give to me this land in which I now dwell. God will bless you and will bring that woman to my son. But if she does not want to come, you shall be clear of this oath." Here can be discerned the second guiding principle for the believer to follow in choosing a mate: go to one's homeland and to one's kindred to obtain one's life-companion.

First, however, let us see and understand here that, spiritually speaking Eliezer the steward represents the Holy Spirit. God decides and purposes a certain matter and it then is the Holy Spirit who will operate to execute and carry out the matter to its rightful conclusion. If as believers we are willing to commit the act of choosing a mate to God our Father, we shall find that the Holy Spirit will become active on our behalf. It is because we do not commit this undertaking to our heavenly Father that the

Holy Spirit has no opportunity to work for us. If you do not commit the choice of your life-companion to God, thus depriving the Holy Spirit the opportunity to work for you, then naturally you will have to work out the matter yourself. How many young people today are working themselves to death in that way! How easily they are misled; how easily they fall into some trap or some snare, from which they cannot extricate themselves. If, however, they would commit this undertaking to their heavenly Father, He would most surely ask the Holy Spirit to become active and work for them in providing the proper mate.

Now with regard to the second guiding principle earlier mentioned, we shall see how Eliezer—symbolizing the Holy Spirit—worked in accordance with that principle which Abraham—representing God the Father—had laid down: he was not to secure a mate for Isaac from among the unbelieving Canaanitish women but he was to go to Abraham's homeland and obtain Isaac's wife from his master's kinfolk. Spiritually speaking, therefore, when a Christian brother or sister is looking for a mate, wherein will the Holy Spirit carry out His work? We must recognize and acknowledge that God has ordained for us believers a boundary or scope within which only there will the Holy Spirit search out a mate for us. If you try searching for your life-companion beyond that scope, the Holy Spirit will not be there searching for you. The scope or parameter is clear: you are to go to your homeland and among your brethren exclusively. In spiritual terms, this narrative in Genesis 24 bespeaks the fact that God has set forth a boundary within which believing brothers and sisters can, by the Holy Spirit, look for a life-companion: it is only to be among one's spiritual kindred—that is to say, among believers in the Lord, among those who belong to the family of God—that he or she is to search out and find his or her counterpart.

"Be Not Unequally Yoked with Unbelievers"

In II Corinthians 6 God through Paul has commanded us to adhere to this very principle: "Be not unequally yoked with unbelievers." We who are believers in Christ are exhorted not to be diversely, unequally yoked with *un*believers, because a marriage entered into between a man and a woman constitutes a being yoked or bound together for a lifetime. Why does the Bible admonish us to "not be unequally yoked with unbelievers"? Many reasons are given here in verses 14-16 of this passage of Scripture. Let us consider each one of them carefully.

Our Position

"For what participation is there between righteousness and lawlessness?" This speaks of our position as believers before God: we are righteous before Him. The righteousness of God has come upon us through Christ

Jesus. Indeed, we are clothed with Christ himself as our righteousness (cf. I Corinthians 1:30). Such, then, is our standing or ground or position before God. But so far as the unbelieving people in the world are concerned, they are deemed lawless before God. In His sight their position or ground is a law-breaking or lawless one. And hence, there can be no participation or partnership between these two.

Our Daily Conduct

"What fellowship [is there] of light with darkness?" So far as our daily conduct as Christians is concerned, we walk in the light as God is in the light. We thus have fellowship one with another, and the blood of Jesus Christ, God's Son, cleanses us from all our sins (I John 1:7). But so far as the behavior of the world's people is concerned, they walk in darkness. They are children of darkness and they therefore live and walk in darkness. Thus, there can be no communion or fellowship between these two groups of people.

Our Governing Principle

"And what consent [can there be] of Christ with Belial?" So far as government and authority is concerned, who is governing our life as believers? It is Christ, for He is our Master and Lord. Who, though, is governing the life of the unbelievers? Belial—that is, Satan, the wicked one—is governing them. So even the governing principle of life over these two groups of people is different the one from the other; and hence, there can be no consent, harmony or agreement between the two.

Our Attitude

"Or what part [is there] for a believer along with an unbeliever?" With respect to the issue of one's attitude, we are those who believe; but the world does not believe. So there can be nothing in common between the world of unbelief and us believers.

Our Purpose of Life

"And what agreement [is there] of God's temple with idols? for ye are the living God's temple." Regarding our purpose in life, we Christians are the temple of God. We are here to allow Him to live in and through us because we are here to serve Him. Regarding the people of this world, though, they are actually serving idols. Accordingly, there can be no agreement between God's people and idolaters.

If, then, you are exercised concerning this action of finding your mate, I would strongly urge you not to go to the children of the Canaanites. In other words, do not look for your mate among the unbelievers of the world; rather, look for your life-companion among those who are of the family of God.

In response, some people may perhaps say, "Well, if I search out a mate among unbelievers, I can have the opportunity of saving another soul." In this very regard, one day a sister in the Lord went to that great English preacher, Charles Spurgeon, and asked him: "Is it all right for me to marry an unbeliever?" She went on to explain the reason for her inquiry: "I could bring him to the Lord and another soul could be won to Christ. Would that not be good?" Spurgeon said in response, "All right, let's try something here." There was a table nearby, and so he asked this young sister to climb up and stand on the table. She did not know why he wanted her to do that, but she hearkened to his request and stood on the table. Then Spurgeon stretched out his hand and told her to do the same. So they clasped their hands together while Spurgeon told her: "Now pull." Of course, that sister was unable to pull Spurgeon up onto the table; instead, she was pulled down to the floor by the preacher. Then Spurgeon explained as follows: "Now, if you want to marry an unbeliever, that is what will happen. You may think you can pull him up to where you are in the Lord, but you will be pulled down by him to where he is in the world."

I would therefore beseech you, on the basis of God's word, that in choosing a mate you not go outside the church into the world to find your life-companion. It is

God's will, rather, that you should find that one among believers. Then you both can be equally yoked and can serve the Lord together. How extremely important this is! Many families end up with great tragedies because, from the outset, the one who is a believer had disregarded the clear word of God. The Holy Spirit always and only operates along the line of God's word. Therefore, you cannot expect Him to operate and work for you outside the boundary of God's word; but you *can* expect the Spirit to operate on your behalf if you obey the word of God.

The Place of Grace

Notice how this servant went about finding the mate for his master's son. In the city of Nahor there were many virgin women who were not yet married. The servant was a stranger to that city. How, then, was he going to find a wife for Isaac in the city of Nahor? When he arrived at that city he decided to go to one particular place: he went to that city's well. In those olden days there would usually be a well located either just outside the city or in the city square. Invariably there would be a well because the community's populace must have water to drink. Moreover, that well was the place in those days to where the womenfolk would go with their pitchers for the purpose of drawing water to take to their homes. So when this servant came to Nahor, he knew where to go to find women: he went to that well and had his camels kneel down. Then he began to pray, "Lord, God of my master Abraham, prosper me. When the women come here to draw their needful water, I shall ask a woman for a drink; and if she not only gives *me* drink but also gives drink to my many camels, then I shall know that this is the woman You have chosen for my master's son." Now before he had even ended praying, behold, a certain woman, Rebecca by name, appeared at the well.

Let us pause to consider this: What, in spiritual terms, does the place of the *well* represent? In the Scriptures a well always betokens divine grace; for out of the well comes forth water and, spiritually speaking, that points to living water, which is to say, the Spirit of life which is God's grace towards mankind (Ezekiel 47:1-12; Zechariah 14:8; John 4:6-7, 10, 13-14; 7:37-39; Revelation 22:1-2). So where in the city of Nahor will this servant go to find grace for his master? He will go to that city's well because that is the place where the women will make their appearance. In spiritual terms according to the New Testament, therefore, we can say that the place of the well is where Christian believers gather together. We Christians assemble together around the Lord—the place of grace—in order to receive grace from God. Hence, this is the place the believer in Christ should go to find a mate. You do not go to a dance hall to find your mate; you do not go to a cinema to discover your mate; you do not go to a race course to secure your mate; you surely do not go to a political rally to obtain your mate; you do not even go to a secular social gathering to find your mate. Instead, you go to the church, to the place where God's people come to draw living water—to where God's people congregate for the purpose of drawing upon the life of God. *That* is the proper place where you shall discover your life-companion.

So here we observe that this servant was most clever and wise. He did not go to any other place than that city's well, even though there were so many women in Nahor. He did not knock on every house door in the community; instead, he simply positioned himself at the city's well and prayed. He committed the entire affair to God and looked for Him to prosper his mission.

If you are one who is looking for a life-partner, trust the Holy Spirit to guide and lead you; but for this to occur you will need to go to the right place for searching out your future spouse. Do not go to the many and varied venues of the world to try to discover your counterpart but you must go among God's gathered people. And as you yourself gather with them and learn to serve together, God will reveal to you who your life-counterpart is to be. Just pray and commit the matter to Him.

Two Extremes

Let us be aware that we can make this endeavor of choosing a mate either so spiritual or so human. We can go to either of these two extremes. Some people make choosing a mate so completely human that they leave God out of the picture entirely. They most likely reason within themselves as follows: "Well, it is my need. It is a physical necessity and therefore a thing of this world. I am the one who is to choose my mate." So they simply go forth and become very active in finding a life-partner on their own. And if they cannot find one in the church, they will seek to discover one in the world: they will attend all kinds of social gatherings in order to have more opportunities to choose. They become very actively involved in searching out and choosing a mate on their own, but they never go to the *proper* place and never pray. Now that can be one extreme.

But we can go to the other extreme of becoming too spiritual in this matter of choosing a life-companion: we approach the matter in a super-spiritual or pseudo-spiritual manner. That is to say, you who are seeking a mate will commit the matter to the Lord for Him to choose while you merely sit around and end up being very passive: you do not lift a finger to cooperate with the Holy Spirit. That approach is far too spiritual. Let us realize that in *all* spiritual affairs we need to be passively active. Whether it is in reading the Scriptures, whether it is in our daily activities, or whether it is in choosing a mate, our attitude must always be one of being passively active. In the present circumstance it means that we need to commit the choosing of a mate to God and then be constantly alert to the leading of His Holy Spirit and learn to cooperate with Him.

Character

Let us return to Abraham's servant once again. He prayed: "When the women come out to draw water, if I say to a woman, 'Give me to drink . . .'" Bear in mind that he had had no intention of asking *every* woman. He could have stayed there by the well and have asked hundreds of women because in that city hundreds of them would have probably been coming out every day to draw water. Had the servant asked every woman, he would have become very confused. No, he prayed: "Lord, I will watch. When the women appear, I will simply watch. Then I will ask one specific woman." Eliezer only asked a woman after engaging in observation. It is just here that the act of choosing a mate comes into play. On the one hand, you who are looking for a mate commit the matter to God. Your heart is open to Him. You only want what He wants for you. And if you have that kind of attitude and are praying, then on the other hand, you watch. You do not ask just anyone, nor do you ask everyone, but when a certain someone comes along and you somehow feel at liberty to ask, then you ask.

You might say, of course, that in following that procedure, you obviously will be judging more or less by the *outward* appearance; and I would probably agree. But let us understand that outward appearance can reveal more than one might think. The servant was certainly not simply looking for a fair lady and nothing more. On the contrary, a fair countenance will no doubt be a point of consideration, but by the very manner or way a woman acts, one can discern a great deal more. So the servant did not engage in asking everyone who came along; instead, he watched and observed. From the very outset that was to be his intention. He would only ask a woman in whom he sensed there was something especially commendable.

If we become so emotionally involved, we shall be blind to those less favorable traits in a potential mate. But if we can stand by and watch what God will do by His Spirit, then we can afford to be more observant. Naturally, it being God who was at work here, He answered Eliezer's prayer quickly: "Behold, Rebecca came." God brought Rebecca to him. She was of fair countenance and, having never known a man, she was a virgin. How did the servant know this? In himself the servant could not and did not know. Yet God knew. Eliezer only knew that she was of fair countenance, but as he watched, he sensed there was a positive potential there. There must have been something commendable in Rebecca and not that she merely possessed a fair countenance. To this servant there must have been something more revealing, perhaps discernible in her very manner. Hence, when she drew water for herself, the servant quickly went forward and asked her to give him a little water to drink out of her pitcher.

Let us now notice what Rebecca did. She hurriedly took down her pitcher and said to Eliezer, "Drink, and I will also draw water for your camels until they have drunk their fill." And immediately she began to draw water for pouring into a trough that was there from which the camels could drink. Now Eliezer had ten camels as his beasts of burden for the journey. These camels of his had walked hundreds of miles on this servant's wilderness journey, and thus they had to have been quite thirsty. In fact, to satisfy the thirst of ten camels, the woman had to draw *much* water! To give drink to an elderly man like Eliezer was a simple matter, but to provide drink for ten thirsty camels was going to be quite a task; for camels can drink, and drink, and drink. And after their immense thirst has finally been quenched, they then proceed to store even more water within those humps of theirs for going on yet another long journey.

What this woman did in giving drink to a total stranger showed kindness on her part; yet let us note that her kindness and compassion extended not only to man but even to animals—and animals of a sort which would require a great deal of work on her part. This betokened to Eliezer the kind of character in this woman which he was looking for in choosing a mate for his master's son. Indeed, this servant was on the lookout for something more attractive than just the outward physical consideration involved in choosing a mate for Isaac. Most certainly the woman to be chosen should be of a fair countenance and not repulsive in appearance. Abraham's servant, however, was looking for something more than that: he was looking for *character.*

For a woman to be a proper wife, she has to be compassionate, kind, and generous; she also has to be friendly, hospitable, and diligent. Now all these are character traits. And these character traits are very, very important for anyone to consider when in search for a life-companion. And such was what Eliezer was pleased to notice in the character of Rebecca. For instance, he had to have noticed how diligent she was. She was not trying to get by with undertaking as little work as possible. To the contrary, Rebecca was not afraid to work but was willing to do so; briefly put, she was most diligent. Moreover, she was very kind, generous, and hospitable. This servant, therefore, had no hesitation in concluding that this woman would be a good counterpart for his master's son Isaac.

Let us again pause for a moment, this time to ponder the second part of Proverbs 31 which is most apt here in relation to what has just been said about Rebecca. It is a Scripture passage that is most beautiful. I hope all brethren present will read it many times, especially the young brothers and sisters. There you will find described a woman of exceeding worth. What kind of woman is she? She is described as being diligent, kind, and generous. She is one who stretches "out her hand to the afflicted" and reaches "forth her hands to the needy." In addition, she opens "her mouth with wisdom" and "upon her tongue is the law of kindness." Moreover, she surveys "the ways of her household and does not eat the bread of idleness." Furthermore, "her children rise up and call her blessed," and her husband likewise praises her: "Many daughters have done worthily, but thou excellest them all. Gracefulness is deceitful and beauty is vain; [but] a woman that feareth Jehovah, she shall be praised." Now this is a portrait of praiseworthy character (vv. 10-31).

Therefore, with regard to this matter of choosing a mate, there are to be not only certain physical attributes which you should observe but also the inward beauty: those commendable inner character qualities. Such is very, very essential for you to take into account when choosing your counterpart for life. Whether it be the case of your looking for the right man or looking for the right woman, certain positive character traits are extremely important for your potential life-companion to possess.

The Spirit of Worship

All the time at the well the servant simply stood there and watched. He simply watched how God, to whom he had prayed for a prosperous outcome, would work towards the fulfillment of his mission. And when everything was finished, Eliezer brought out one gold ring and two gold bracelets and gave them to the woman and inquired: "What is your name? What family do you come from? Is there any place for me, my servants, and the camels to lodge?"

Rebecca answered that she came from the very family of Abraham, that of the family of Nahor his relative. She also said that there would be plenty of space and provision in her home. And Eliezer, upon hearing all these words, bowed down and worshiped God. Throughout this entire Genesis narrative it can readily be observed that the spirit of that servant was a spirit of worship.

We too often think that we believers worship God only when we come together on Sunday morning. Not so! You can and ought to worship God even throughout the entire process of finding your mate of God's choice. Do not make the matter of choosing one's life-partner such a secular affair that it has no relation to the act of worship. Quite the contrary, if you commit this entire endeavor to God and look to the Holy Spirit for its fulfillment, if you truly walk in His way, you will see how the Spirit of God will work on your behalf and you will be just like Abraham's servant who simply stood by and watched how the entire process played itself out. And the result will be that it will draw out continual worship from you during the whole process: indeed, every step will draw out worship. How much, if any at all, of our mating process draws out worship today? I would venture to say, Not much. Yet this is what should be the result: the entire process should prompt from us the continual act of worship because of our witnessing the divine working out of God's very own purpose. Oh, how beautiful that must be!

A Complete Union

A further point on the subject at hand needs to be mentioned and stressed. Which is, that the union of a man and a woman is not merely to be a physical one but is to be a total union of spirit and soul and body between two human beings. And because it is to be a complete union, therefore, in choosing a mate for oneself all *three* elements making up human beings (cf. I Thessalonians 5:23b) should be carefully considered and not just the physical one.

Today, unfortunately, many young people take into account only the physical side when choosing a mate. And with respect to this side, they only consider one aspect of it: Is the man handsome? Is the woman beautiful? That is the end all and be all in their consideration. But Proverbs 31 tells us that "gracefulness is deceitful and beauty is vain; [but] a woman that feareth Jehovah, she shall be praised" (v. 30). Well, of course, physical attraction is a factor to be considered; that is true. As was indicated earlier, at the very least there should not be repulsion towards one's future mate, for if there is, how can two people possibly come together? There must therefore be present in one's future mate a certain degree of physical attraction.

But that does not constitute the full extent of one's consideration of the physical side to the union of a man and woman in marriage. Not only is there the factor of attraction but that of health should be taken into account as well. Also, the aspect of heredity should be considered since it could adversely affect the second generation. Then, too, family background ought to be included when contemplating the physical side in one's choice of a mate. Yet not in the sense of the old Chinese tradition which calls for you to find a mate possessing "the same doors" as those of yourself—in other words, according to this tradition both of you must have the same social status, the same wealth, and so forth. That requirement is too worldly; nevertheless, certain family background considerations are important to inquire after since a difference in lifestyles between two mates could be a source of conflict later if one spouse or the other finds it too difficult to change his or her previously developed lifestyle. Hence, one or the other's family background should be looked at very carefully when contemplating marriage. And of course, the matter of age should likewise not be overlooked. Hence, all these various factors relating to the physical side should be brought before God most carefully.

However, any contemplated union between a man and a woman in marriage will not involve merely a union of two physical bodies; it must also involve a union of two souls; and therefore, the psychological side ought also to be carefully weighed and considered. In other words, in choosing one's partner for life, a person needs to consider the issue of character—do you discern in the man or woman, as the case may be, that basic qualitative character which is vital for a family to have? In addition, you need to know whether or not there is companionableness in the other person: some individuals are so "by themselves" that they are unable to live with other people. In choosing a mate this is a most serious matter which needs to be addressed. Then, too, the moral and ethical aspects of life together must be inquired after in the other person: Where does he or she stand in relation to these kinds of issues? Is he or she likely to be faithful, loyal, trustworthy, and honest?

Naturally, added to these two sides in the union will be the spiritual side. First, the other person must, of course, be a believer. Second, both parties to any marriage union must love God. Though people may be believers, some may have no heart for Him. If you yourself have a heart for God but the other person does not, you will find such a believer very difficult to get along with later because a Christian family is supposed to serve God together. Unless you both are of one mind, of one heart, and of one love towards God, how can the two of you serve Him together? Should the husband wish to serve God but the wife does not, or if the wife desires to serve

God but the husband does not, and even if they are both believers, you will discover to your great sorrow immense difficulties arising. It is most essential, therefore, that both potential spouses not only be believers but that both also love God and wish to serve Him together.

When all the above aspects of body, soul, and spirit are considered in a positive, favorable light, such can rightfully be the basis for realizing a total union of two human beings. And hence, this process of choosing a mate according to God's will and way is not an insignificant matter.

The Perfect, Ideal Mate—Not Possible

One last word. Generally speaking, young people have very high ideals. You as a young man or woman are looking for an ideal counterpart to be with you for life. Accordingly, you will most likely establish for yourself a very high standard and will then want to find a person who will measure up perfectly to that standard of yours—one hundred percent. Let me frankly tell you straight out: you will not find such a person on this earth! On the one hand, you do need to see that God has set forth in His word certain principles by which you need to walk; but on the other hand, you must not attempt to find the perfect, ideal mate. Such an attempt will only end in failure:

you won't obtain the perfect him or her as your life-companion.

By way of conclusion, when all these various basic principles and points are considered, and as you put this entire endeavor before God, He will exercise your heart; and if He grants you a "go-ahead," then go forward. And may this brief discussion on the subject of choosing a mate, whose principles we find in the Scriptures, be helpful to those who have yet to establish a family for themselves.

Our heavenly Father, we do thank Thee because Thou art the One who dost create the need and desire and dost provide the supply. We praise and thank Thee that from the very beginning to the very end we can see Thy hand working by Thy Spirit, and so we can maintain an attitude of prayer and worship. Oh God, we do pray for the young people among us and among Thy people everywhere. Oh, we do pray that Thou wouldst give the young people a desire to seek Thy face in this matter of mating. We pray Thou wilt sovereignly bring the partners of Thy *choice together so that families may be established on a solid Biblical ground and that they may be a building block for Thy church. We give Thee all the praise and glory. In the name of our Lord Jesus. Amen.*

Chapter Five
Husband and Wife Relationship

Ephesians 5:22-33—Wives, submit yourselves to your own husbands, as to the Lord, for a husband is head of the wife, as also the Christ is head of the assembly. He is Saviour of the body. But even as the assembly is subjected to the Christ, so also wives to their own husbands in everything. Husbands, love your own wives, even as the Christ also loved the assembly, and has delivered himself up for it, in order that he might sanctify it, purifying it by the washing of water by the word, that he might present the assembly to himself glorious, having no spot, or wrinkle, or any of such things; but that it might be holy and blameless. So ought men also to love their own wives as their own bodies; he that loves his own wife loves himself. For no one has ever hated his own flesh, but nourishes and cherishes it, even as also the Christ the assembly: for we are members of his body; we are of his flesh, and of his bones. Because of this a man shall leave his father and mother, and shall be united to his wife, and the two shall be one flesh. This mystery is great, but I speak as to Christ, and as to the assembly. But ye also, every one of you, let each so love his own wife as himself; but as to the wife I speak that she may fear [reverence] the husband.

Colossians 3:18-19—Wives, be subject to your husbands, as is fitting in the Lord. Husbands, love your wives, and be not bitter against them.

I Peter 3:1-7—Likewise, wives, be subject to your own husbands, that, even if any are disobedient to the word, they may be gained without the word by the conversation [conduct] of the wives, having witnessed your pure conversation carried out in fear; whose adorning let it not be that outward one of tressing of hair, and wearing gold, or putting on apparel; but the hidden man of the heart, in the incorruptible ornament of a meek and quiet spirit, which in the sight of God is of great price. For thus also the holy women who have hoped in God heretofore adorned themselves, being subject to their own husbands; as Sarah obeyed Abraham, calling him lord; whose children ye have become, doing good, and not fearing with any kind of consternation. Ye husbands likewise, dwell with them according to knowledge, as with a weaker, even the female, vessel, giving them honour, as also fellow-heirs of the grace of life, that your prayers be not hindered.

We have already come to see that the family is a divine—not a human—concept. God originates the family, and the latter is for the purpose of fulfilling His will and plan. So God originates the family by creating man as both male and female and then joining them into one. And thus the first family—that of Adam and Eve—is formed. Moreover, to that family God gave a very important task: to multiply and fill the earth and subdue it. In other words, God wished to use that first family to restore the earth, which had been ruined by His angelic enemy Satan, back to himself so that He might be glorified in all things.

However, with the fall of man in the Edenic garden a grievous development occurred within that original family: instead of it being a God-centered family it became a self-centered one, with even a separation having occurred between husband and wife: Eve was alone away from her husband, which helped to usher in the fall of mankind. Moreover, this family would eventually manifest a lack of love, and of course there was also a violation of God's divine order: instead of Adam remaining the head of the family his wife was now observed taking the lead.

Even so, we earlier also came to see that when God commenced His work of redemption for fallen mankind, He included the family in His redemptive plan: if we believe in His Son Jesus, we *individually* shall be saved but also our *households* will too. And, as we learned in our last discussion together, in order for a Christian family to be established, the process towards its fulfillment must begin with believers in the Lord finding and choosing the right partner through the help of God's Holy Spirit. And today, I would like for us to consider together a further subject area in our continuing discussion concerning God's purpose for the family; namely, the relationship between the husband and the wife in the Christian family.

Now the fundamental constituent elements of the family are, of course, the husband and the wife. God brings a man and a woman together that they may be one. They share the same physical life, for we all have received from our forefathers the same physical or human life. Not only that, even their spiritual life is the same, because we are assuming here that both the husband and the wife are believers in the Lord Jesus. Therefore, the apostle Peter writes in his first epistle that the husband and the wife are "fellow-heirs of the grace of life." So far as their spiritual life is concerned, they are fellow heirs: they are equal partners. There is no passage in the Bible which tells us that either the man or the woman is or must be more spiritual than the other. In relation to spiritual life the man and the woman—husband and wife—are equals. But for the sake of the smooth, efficient functioning of the family, God in fact sets the husband as the head of the family and sets the wife as the body of the family.

We would like to look at this subject of the husband-and-wife relationship from three different aspects: 1) the position and responsibility of the husband in the family as well as that of the wife; 2) how one should be a husband and how one should be a wife in the family—all according to God's word; and 3) how the husband and the wife should adjust to each other.

Position and Responsibility

It has already been pointed out that with regard to their life the husband and the wife are equal. But with regard to the functioning or operation of the family, God has established a particular order therein. The fact of God's ordaining this order in the family has absolutely nothing to do with equality or inequality; He has done it simply for the sake of efficiency. Positionally, God sets the husband to be the head of the family; and naturally, as the family's head, there will be certain responsibilities involved. On the other hand, positionally, God has also set the wife as the body of the family; and as the family's body, she likewise must assume certain responsibilities. The working together of the husband and wife in accordance with this divine order will build the family up most beautifully before God.

Divine Order

Now in approaching this subject of order, I believe we must hearken back to the very first appearance of divine order in the universe and what characterized or inspired it. If the divine order is to be established in reality in a given Christian family, it cannot come about simply by declaring it so—beginning with the husband and wife. In other words, if it is declared to the wife, "Wife, you must submit to your husband," the wife will probably retort: "He is no more spiritual than I am; why, then, should I submit myself to him?" Or if it is declared to the husband, "Husband, you are to be the head of the family," the husband will most likely respond: "Well, now! That is far too much responsibility for me to handle." The divine order between the husband and the wife can never begin to be realized in such fashion; on the contrary, if the divine order is truly to be established in the family it can only be brought about if and when the two life-partners see and sincerely embrace the heart and spirit that was inherent at the very inception of divine order.

God: the Head of Christ

> *I wish you to know that the Christ is the head of every man, but woman's head is the man, and the Christ's head God (I Corinthians 11:3).*

Let us see that within the divine order the first feature is that God is the Head of Christ: it all begins with God who is the Head of Christ. Unless each party to a marriage sees this, it will be extremely difficult to have God's order in the family established. From Philippians 2 we learn that the Son and the Father are one. Because the Son is equal with the Father it is not necessary in the least for the Son to grasp after that equality (v. 6). He and the Father share all things: the same life, the same Spirit, the same purpose. In everything They are equal and They are one. Nevertheless, for the sake of God's eternal purpose, plan, and work, the Son most willingly and voluntarily—out of love for the Father—emptied himself of the glory and the honor, the power and position He had with the Father (v.7a). Indeed, the Son did not do this out of any sense of compulsion nor because He was commanded to do it but did so purely out of His love for the Father. Yet let it be clear that in laying aside the exalted privileges of His, Jesus did not empty himself of His deity but only set aside all privileges of honor, position and glory so that He might take the lowest possible form and status of humanity—that of a slave. And being in the form of a man, He humbled himself and was totally obedient to the Father: even to the extremity of death, and *that* the death of a cross (vv. 7b-8). In brief, then, it can be said that so far as life is concerned, the Father and the Son are one and equal; yet out of love and obedience towards the Father, the Son gladly and voluntarily took a much lower position for the sake of God's eternal purpose.

We can also state this matter in another way. When Christ Jesus the Son was on earth, He took the position of being the body and honoring His Father as the Head in all things. By carefully reading the Gospel according to John we discover the Lord Jesus stating again and again this truth concerning himself: "The Son can say and do nothing of and by himself." He repeatedly declared: "I can neither say nor do anything unless I have heard the Father say it or have seen the Father do it" (5:17, 19-21, 25-26, 30, 36b; 7:16-17; 8:28; 12:49-50; 14:10, 24, 31b). In other words, throughout Jesus' entire earthly life He honored His Father as the Head. He never lifted up *His* head nor tried to act on His own. Instead, He willingly submitted himself to the Father as the Head and maintained Himself as the body in all things and in every situation.

Notice, for example, His encounter with the devil out in the desert after having fasted there for forty days and nights. In every challenge the enemy put to Jesus, what did He do? what was His reaction? He held fast to the position of the Father as the Head and himself as the body when He was tempted by Satan in the matter of physical hunger: "If You are the Son of God, turn these stones into bread." Indeed, Jesus at that moment was quite hungry and as the Son of *God* He certainly could turn stones into bread. But Jesus, maintaining himself at a lower position as the Son of *man,* replied: "Man shall not live by bread alone, but by every word that proceeds from the mouth of God" (see Matthew 4:1-4). In other words, in the heart and mind of the Son, the Father is the Head. Jesus' attitude was: "Unless the Father decides that I should turn these desert stones into bread, I will not do it. I would rather remain hungry; I won't do it." His whole life on earth was marked and governed by this one overarching principle: He was obedient to the Father; He held fast the Father as the Head. So to the Son the Father was His Head.

What, though, was the Son to the Father? He was the body to the Father. You may recall one of the themes of Psalm 40 which declares what Jesus, when coming into this world, had said to His Father: "Sacrifices, burnt offerings, oblations You do not want; but behold, You have prepared for Me a body. Lo, I come to do Your will,

O God" (see vv. 6-8 Septuagint; Hebrews 10:5-7). Here we see the relationship between the Father and the Son: the Father is the Head; the Son is the body: the Son offered himself completely as a body to the Father to do the Father's will. How marvelous this divine order is! Such a perfect order between God and Christ. And because of that, the Son not only sets an example for us but also becomes the very power source enabling us to enter into and keep the divine order which God has set among us.

Christ: the Head of Man

The second feature within the divine order as set forth in this same verse in I Corinthians 11 is that Christ is the Head "of every man." Now in the New Testament's original Greek text the English word translated in the Darby Bible as man here is not the same Greek word used to distinguish the human male from the human female. Instead, the word man here in the Greek original actually signifies *mankind*; meaning, therefore, that Christ is the Head of *all* human beings—including both males and females. Hence, with respect to this divine order, we first must see that God is the Head of Christ. Then, second, we must see and enter into the reality of Christ being the Head of all mankind. Especially must every *believer* see this.

When people believe in the Lord Jesus, they receive Him as their personal Savior and, thank God, they are saved. But that is only part of God's salvation. In believing the Lord Jesus you need to not only receive Him as your Savior that you may be saved, you need to also accept Him as your Lord that you may obey Him in all things.

Now saying that you receive Jesus Christ as your Lord can be stated another way: that you receive Him as your Head. Before you believe in the Lord Jesus you are your own head in all matters of life because you do all things according to *your* pleasure. After you have been saved and redeemed, however, you are not your own anymore. How should you then live on this earth? There is henceforth but one proper way you can live: you surrender your life to Christ and say, "Lord, from now on, You are the Head and I am to be the body for doing Your will. Whatever You say, it shall be done. It is now up to You to make clear to me Your will. You are my Head."

Have we all come to this place of surrender yet? Yes, we have believed in the Lord Jesus as our Savior, but have we accepted Him as the Head of every man? Is it true that Christ is your Head—that in all things you are holding fast the reality that Christ is your Head? Or is it the case that *you* are making plans, that *you* are scheming, that *you* are desiring—all for the purpose of simply pleasing yourself? If so, then you have yet to arrive at that place of surrender in your life which calls forth the attitude of heart that impels you to sincerely declare: "Lord, not my will, but Yours be done. What do You want with me? I am here for Your will and pleasure alone. That and that alone is what

I am here for; I am the body, You are the Head." Now this should be true with every believer in Christ, both men *and* women included. Christ is the Head of all of mankind.

The Husband: Head of the Family

Let us acknowledge that the reason the divine order in many Christian families is not established is because, first of all, one or both spouses do not see with spiritual eyes the vision of Christ, how He takes God as His Head. Second of all, that though husband and wife are saved they have not yet surrendered to Christ as the Head of their lives. It is no use saying, "Husband, be head of the family; wife, be the body of the family," if people do not see that the establishing of the divine order in the family stems from that original relationship which exists between Christ and God. That relationship is the very source from whence the supply of power for establishing such a family order emanates. Unless both the man and the woman surrender their lives to God and allow the Lord Jesus to be Head of each of them, there is neither motivation nor way to set up the divine order in the family.

Let me reiterate that the reason the divine order is not established in the family is because, first, either the husband or the wife, or both of them, do not take Christ as their Head. And second, they do not see that God is the Head of Christ. Hence, for God's order in the family to be set up, the parties to the family need to see that just as Christ takes God as His Head so Christ must be Head over all mankind—in the present case, over both the husband and the wife. It is only when, by God's grace and power, both marriage partners have taken Christ as their Head that the husband can be the head of the family and the wife can be the body of the family.

It is not difficult at all for the divine order to be established in the family if both the husband and the wife truly see and hold fast the reality of Christ as their Head. And if that be true of them, then the husband, for example, will not want to do things according to his will, seeking to impose himself upon his wife; rather, he holds fast Christ as his Head by manifesting the attitude: "Lord, what is Your will for the family? I simply wish to carry out what You want." The wife, too, will wish to act in the same way. She will look to the Lord and pray: "Lord, what do You want me to do in the family? It is for You and not for myself." For God's order to be established in the family it has to come into existence in this way.

Responsibilities of the Husband

As we have seen, God sets up the husband to be head of the family. Yet to be its head is not a matter of sitting high up and giving commands but is the undertaking of a great responsibility. In at least three significant areas the husband has to take responsibility as head of the family.

Support of the Family

The first area of responsibility for the husband is that of finance. As head of the family he should provide the necessary income support. After the fall of man God had said to Adam: "From now on you have to toil and sweat in order to earn a living." When God said that to Adam, however, He was not saying it with only him in mind but was declaring it with Adam's family in mind as well. Adam was to toil and to sweat in order to earn a living for himself and for his family—that is to say, he was to take care of his wife and children. As the head of the family, the husband is responsible for supporting it.

Today, here in the United States, many husbands and wives are both out working. I readily agree at the outset of this discussion that there are family situations which call for exceptions; nevertheless, it cannot be denied that God's way is that the responsibility of supporting the family should rest solely upon the shoulders of the husband. If the husband cannot himself provide the necessary support, it will become very difficult for him to be the head of the family. True, in certain situations there may be legitimate reasons for both the husband and the wife to work in order to support the family. But I wonder if in today's so-called modern families one reason why both husband and wife must work is perhaps due to their desire to compete favorably with some other family's lifestyle. It is my belief that Christians should live on a much simpler scale. A simple lifestyle is more conducive to one's spiritual growth. Today, life has become so complicated. People feel the need to constantly raise their standard of living. They feel compelled that they compete with their neighbors. And because of that, the husband alone cannot support the family. If, however, the family lifestyle were simpler, it could very well be possible for that husband to do so. But since the family does not live more simply, it obviously requires that both the husband and the wife work in order to support the family, even though it may be assumed that the wife already has a full-time job in the home caring for the children and carrying out other responsibilities. And the sad result is that the family suffers.

Let me acknowledge again that there *are* exceptions. At times, and even though a family may indeed be pursuing a very simple lifestyle, the husband is still unable by himself to earn enough to support the family. In that case the wife will naturally have to help out. Nevertheless, in most instances the divine order would call for the husband as the family head to assume sole responsibility of financially supporting his household so that the wife could devote herself to a most vital family task: caring for the children.

Government of the Family

As the head of the family the husband must carry out a second area of responsibility: that of making policy decisions. In other words, the government of the family is to be exercised by the husband. The making of key policy decisions for governing the family—such as the lifestyle to be adopted, the direction in which the family should go, etc.—is the responsibility of the husband. However, this does not mean that he can make a given decision without consulting his wife, for it must not be forgotten that they are partners. The husband, therefore, should not simply proceed to make a decision on his own and then inform his wife of it and ask her to act accordingly. That would be despotic. Instead, the husband should consult his wife by sharing and talking over the matter together; even so, the final decision should, and does in fact, rest with the husband as the head of the family, who will then expect his wife to carry it out.

Spiritual Welfare of the Family

Reading the Old Testament reveals the fact that back then the father of the family was usually the priest of the household. Consider Job, for example. Even after his children were married and had their own families, whenever those grown-up children of his were feasting together, he would offer up sacrifices to God on their behalf the following morning (1:4-5). One could also mention Abraham, and many others. This indicates that as head of the family the husband is responsible for its spiritual welfare. Today, unfortunately, many husbands are not performing that duty; instead, they are leaving that task to the wives. We must thank God for these faithful wives; nevertheless, the husbands as family heads are supposed to lead in caring for the spiritual welfare of their families.

Therefore, in at least these three areas of responsibility the husband is to take the lead in his capacity as head of the family.

Responsibilities of the Wife

In her capacity as the body the wife plays a supporting role in the family whereas the husband plays the leading role. Even so, she, too, has three main areas of responsibility. Let us take up each one of them here.

Managing the Finances

With respect to the family's finances, the wife—though according to God's divine order she is not required to help in bringing in the family income—will most likely be the one who *manages* the finances. After all, she is actually the one most involved in using the money. And if she uses the finances wisely, it will result in the building up of the family.

Increasingly today in modern societies there are husbands who must hold down two jobs (in fact, I know of some who must hold down three). Some husbands even pursue illegal ways of gaining money. And why? Because their wives have such excessive desires and ambitions. Whether the wives are spendthrifts or thrifty ones, whether they are wasteful or frugal, such outcomes—whether for good or ill—will affect the family very much. The wife, in her role as manager of the family's finances, is to spend the money most carefully for the necessities of the family. Let us again notice that virtuous wife described in Proverbs 31: how she makes good use of the family's money and even earns profit from it; and hence none in her family has any need (vv. 16, 18a, 24). As the body of the family the wife is to make use most wisely the money which has come in for the family.

Managing the Family

The second area of responsibility—the management of the family—also rests upon the wife. As we saw earlier, whereas it is the husband who makes the decision on certain policies, it is the wife who carries them out. Likewise, when it comes to the family's myriad daily affairs—buying food, dressing the children, the thousand and one other things to be done in the family—it is actually the wife who manages all such matters. She is in truth the family's manager. In her supporting role as the body of the family, the wife carries out the policies which have been laid down by the husband as head with respect to the lifestyle and the direction of the family.

Bringing Up the Children

The third area falls along the spiritual line: the wife is to assist the husband in bringing up the children in the admonition and the discipline of the Lord. When the husband is away, she must step in and fill the gap. There is more I could say about this area, but I must hasten on to other matters in our discussion for today.

In the family, then, we can see that the husband has certain responsibilities as the head and the wife has certain responsibilities as the body. And if the divine order is present and functioning properly, these two partners shall work together for the building up of their family before God.

How to Be a Husband Or Wife

Our dear brother Watchman Nee once offered up the following remarks before an audience of believers: "If anyone wants to be a nurse, it requires certain years of schooling and training. If anyone wants to be an engineer, he too has to pursue years of study and training. If anyone wants to be a doctor, he likewise must undertake many years of study and practical training as an intern. In other words, every job one might choose requires training. If you are not properly prepared and trained, you are not able to take the job and do it well. Is it not strange, however, that when a man and a woman are married, it is assumed that without any schooling or training the man instantly knows how to be a husband and the woman immediately knows how to be a wife? Somehow because they are thrust into that *particular* position of husband or wife, they automatically know how to be a husband and how to be a wife. No wonder there are so many inadequate husbands and wives. They have never learned how! If a husband and a wife should really set their minds to learning how, perhaps after five years they might be successful."

Well now, I think brother Nee had wanted to impress upon his audience that we cannot take things for granted. For you to become a partner in marriage and raise a family is the most important job of your life; yet you are practically without any preparation or training! Oh, how husbands and wives need to be before God about this matter. If we as husbands and wives are willing to come before Him concerning such lack, then by His mercy and grace we may end up being successful in His eyes.

Actually, in the Bible there are teachings and instructions on how to be a husband and how to be a wife. We invariably deem the Letters to the Ephesians and the Colossians as being two of the most spiritual books in the entire Bible. Why is this our reaction? It is because the Letter to the Ephesians speaks of the church as the body of Christ and the Letter to the Colossians speaks of Christ as the Head of the body—the church. These two Bible books reach to the summit, as it were, of spiritual revelation. Yet within the text of these two highly spiritual epistles of Paul's we also find practical, common-sense instructions on how to be a husband and how to be a wife. And how very much down to earth these instructions are. Spirituality is not some ethereal element floating somewhere in the air; spirituality, for it to be such, has to be manifested in terms of practical living—even as we find in these two Pauline letters. We also find this in the First Letter of the apostle Peter. The whole theme of I Peter concerns the lofty theme of the kingdom, and yet he too touches upon this practical subject of the husband and the wife. So in these three places of Scripture we are taught and instructed on how to be a husband and how to be a wife.

Now at this moment in our discussion I would like to point out one interesting fact which has continually puzzled me. I do not know for certain why it is that in each of these three Scripture passages God through Paul and Peter is found instructing the wives *first* and then instructing the husbands. I have long pondered this unusual sequential order. As we have previously learned, God's order in the family is for the husband to be the head and the wife to be the body. As we all know, at the very beginning Adam was created first and only later did Eve appear. Why is it, then, that in God's word where instructions are given on how to be a husband and how to be a wife, the divine order for the family seems to have been reversed in all three of these Scripture passages: they first mentioning wives and then the husbands?

It came to me one day that it might possibly be due to the fact that the wives influence the husbands more than the husbands influence the wives. I have wondered ever since if that is the explanation. We will recall that the very first instance of this influence had occurred in the Garden of Eden: it was not Adam who had influenced Eve but Eve who had influenced Adam. Oh, how true and how often, that for the sake of harmony in the family the husband will simply go along with what the wife wants, does, or asserts. Probably it is for this reason that we find the *first* set of instructions which are given in the Scriptures on how to be a husband or wife is that given for the *wives*. Thus leading me to the conclusion that possibly these Biblical writers, as inspired by God's Spirit, had reasoned that if the right wives are established first, it would be easier to obtain the right husbands. Let me state again, however, that I am not at all certain about this; I simply offer this explanation as one possible solution to the puzzle for anyone interested to consider.

God's Word to Wives

Be that as it may, it can readily be observed that in all three Scripture passages which we have read together today, God's first teaching and/or instruction presented on how to be a proper husband or wife in the family is concerned with the wives. And in all three passages God can be seen emphasizing one factor above all others. In Ephesians we read: "Wives, submit to your own husbands as to the Lord." In Colossians we read: "Wives, be subject to your husbands, for it is fitting in the Lord." And in I Peter we similarly read: "Wives, be subject to your husbands, even if your husband is not the Lord's." Briefly stated, the teaching of the Bible concerning how to be a proper wife is centered on this matter of submission or subjection.

Let us notice that the Bible verses do *not* say, "Wives, *love* your husbands," the lack of *that* kind of instruction thus apparently signifying that in the minds of these Bible writers it is already very natural for wives to love their husbands (and therefore there would be no need for such instruction), though, of course, it is natural love that would be meant. But for wives to be submissive—or, to be subject—to their husbands requires the infusion of *divine* love. Let me say to the wives and to those who may one day become wives: You do indeed have within you a natural love, but in that natural love there is not that element of submissiveness. To demonstrate that you truly love your husband, you need the love of Christ in you, because only in His love is there that element of submissiveness. This element of submission comes forth out of love and not out of command or compulsion or force. So that just as Christ the Son submitted himself to God His Father, even so out of her own will the wife willingly and voluntarily and because of her love towards Christ and towards her husband, submits herself to her husband: she seeks to adapt herself to her husband, seeks to complete and perfect her husband; in fact, she gives up her personal desire in order that she may be submissive to her husband in love.

In the Scriptures submission is depicted as being more an attitude of the heart or mind; hence, submission is the expression of an inner heart attitude. Why submit? To do so is because of the love of Christ. In reality, as a wife submits to her husband she is actually submitting herself to the Lord Jesus. To describe the matter another way, in the present context, unless a wife can see the Lord, she cannot submit. Many wives will say, "Why should I submit to my husband?" Well, if as a wife you truly see the Lord Jesus—how He as the Son submits himself to God in all things—then you will submit yourself to your husband as to Christ. You take the Lord Jesus as your standard—as your example—and allow the life of Christ within you to constrain you in love (see II Corinthians 5:14). That is the only way for Christian wives to be motivated to submit.

Now it is quite true that among non-Christian families people have what could be termed a natural concept which holds that wives should indeed be subject to their husbands. But that is only a moral concept. With regard to Christian families, however, it is more than a moral understanding; it is also a spiritual one, in that the wife submits to her husband because she has a spiritual understanding that in doing so she is likewise submitting herself to the Lord Jesus. In her heart and mind the wife has truly seen the Lord and, thus motivated and supplied within by His submissive life and love towards God the Father, she gladly, willingly and voluntarily submits herself to her husband. It hence is quite different from what occurs in the secular world's families. In the unbelieving world wives, as the apostle Peter has intimated, try to attract and hold their husbands by various outward means: they think that by tressing their hair, wearing jewels, or clothing themselves in rich apparel they can win and hold to themselves the hearts of their husbands. Not so for the Christian wife; she will win her husband's heart by the beauty of "the hidden man of the heart." So to the wives, let it be clearly understood that God has one very important request to make of you—that you subject yourselves to your husbands in love as to His Son the Lord Jesus. For as God said through His servant Paul, this "is fitting in the Lord."

God's Word to Husbands

Now just as it was the case with the wives, in these same three Scripture passages which we earlier read together having to do with how to be a proper husband or wife in the family, God can likewise be seen as emphasizing one factor above all others in relation *to the husbands*—and here it is not the factor of submission but of love. Indeed, it would appear as though it is relatively easy for husbands to submit to their wives; but here the Bible addresses the husbands in Ephesians 5 as follows: "Love your own wives even as Christ loved the church and gave himself up for her." Once again we need to be clear that the type of love cited here is not natural love; rather, the Greek word translated as love in this passage is *agape*—that is, divine love. It is that unconditional, absolute love of Christ Jesus. Unless a husband truly humbles himself before Christ and allows His love to fill and constrain his heart, he cannot love his wife as Christ loved the church. So once more we find that the standard or example to be followed is Christ, and that the supply of the power of love is also Christ. It is not an outcome which is natural but spiritual in nature. The husband is not all the time demanding but is instead giving, just as Christ gave himself up for the church.

If the husband can learn to love and the wife can learn to submit, the husband will not need to tell the wife to submit nor will the wife need to tell the husband to love. In other words, each spouse in the marriage should embrace the relevant word of God for himself or herself and not attempt to impose that word upon the other spouse. If the husband and the wife will each take to heart the word of God that is specifically related to himself or herself, and if each of them will not wait for the other partner to begin doing his or her part but instead both begin to do so themselves, there will be no problem.

The Colossian passage instructs, positively, for "husbands [to] love [their] wives" and, negatively, God through Paul adds one further instruction: Husbands, do not be bitter towards your wives. Now what is the meaning of this latter instruction? It signifies that sometimes husbands can demand too much of their wives. Too often they treat them almost as slaves, and because their wives do not meet all their demands, the husbands become unhappy and even grow bitter towards their wives. Husbands should be more considerate of them because, as Peter pointed out, wives are weaker vessels—in the sense that constitutionally they are different in their make-up. Husbands therefore need to love their wives with sensitivity and be more considerate concerning them. These are just some of the instructions given in Scripture for the husband in the family.

The Need for Adjustment

One important concluding thought needs to be mentioned; which is, that the husband and the wife must learn to adjust to each other. Let us bear in mind the fact that, for two adult people who have experienced years of growing up, habits have become rather fixed. Indeed, they bring to the marriage two heretofore very independent wills. For two grown-ups, therefore, to merge together into one is not going to be an easy undertaking. Accordingly, much adjustment between these two will be necessary for the family to be a success.

In this regard I would like to offer up three observations which may be helpful. First, the family is not a reformatory. What do I mean by this? The husband might very well harbor the notion: "Well, I now have a wife, and I am going to do everything I can to reform her to make her fit for myself." And perhaps the wife may have the same intention: "I am going to change and reform him according to my idea of what a good husband should be." If such notions were to be attempted, both parties would be treating the family as a reformatory. No, the family is not a reformatory; far from it, it is *a melting pot*. How, then, can both partners to a marriage be melted together? The solution is that each one has to be willing to be melted *first*. Each must give up one's self first and not attempt to reform the other; on the contrary, if such occurs, many problems will be the result. Instead, let each spouse be melted first. Both need to deny the self, learn to adjust, and then both can be merged into one.

Second, the family is not a court; it is not a place for arguing who is right and who is wrong, as in a courtroom. No, the family is not a court but a *school,* in which both the man and the woman can learn how to adjust to one another. Oh, there are so many such lessons to be learned by both husband and wife, and there is no place where a person can learn more practical, spiritual lessons along this line than in one's family. Indeed, if I may say so, this is where singles miss out on a wonderful opportunity to learn many helpful lessons of life.

And finally, the family is not a battlefield. Parties to a marriage do not take opposite positions on family matters and battle each other out over them. No, the family is not a battlefield but *a workshop*. Both spouses work together to have the work and purpose of God for the family accomplished. A workshop is what a family should be, and if that be the case, there will be many practical matters which both husband and wife will have to consider and many adjustments which will need to be made.

Our heavenly Father, how we praise and thank Thee because Thy life in us is real, practical, and down to earth. Without Thee we can do nothing, without Thee we do not even know how to be a husband or be a wife. But with Thee all things are possible. Oh, we do cast ourselves upon Thee and pray that by Thy grace and because of Thy life in our families there may be set Thy divine order and that there may be present in our families the Lord's love and His spirit of submission. May He be glorified in all our families and may His church be built. In the name of our Lord Jesus. Amen

Chapter Six
Parents and Children

Ephesians 6:1-4—Children, obey your parents in the Lord, for this is just. Honour thy father and thy mother, which is the first commandment with a promise, that it may be well with thee, and that thou mayest be long-lived on the earth. And ye fathers, do not provoke your children to anger, but bring them up in the discipline and admonition of the Lord.

Colossians 3:20-21—Children, obey your parents in all things, for this is well-pleasing in the Lord. Fathers, do not vex your children, to the end that they be not disheartened.

During our last consideration together in this series of messages concerning God's purpose for the family we dealt at some length with what ought to be the proper relationship between the husband and wife. Today I would like to continue further on yet another and very essential aspect of the Christian family, which is that of parents and children and the right relationship which should exist between them. And the two above-quoted passages of Scripture from the Ephesian and Colossian epistles of the apostle Paul can serve as the focus for our discussion together on this important topic.

Now in the Bible there are many instructions and teachings on how to be proper parents and children. For instance, in the Old Testament book of Proverbs can be found many sayings and proverbs which are related to parents and children. In that book there are probably more words spoken to the children than to the parents; yet even to the parents, not a few. And though, as was pointed out last time, the New Testament epistles of Colossians and Ephesians deal with the highest truths one can ever find in the Bible—those revealing, respectively, the church as the body of Christ and Christ as the Head of the body, the church—even so, in these same two epistles Paul is seen giving teachings and instructions concerning not only husbands and wives but also children and parents. We can notice as well that the weight of these teachings/instructions seems to be laid heavier on the parents than on the children.

Furthermore, as has been said before, the Bible is not only spiritual but also very practical. Accordingly, the more spiritual God's people are—the more that they are in the spirit of Christ—the more the life of Christ shall be manifested in the daily human relationships on earth.

Emphasis on Fathers

Married Christians need to realize that to be a husband and a wife only affects one generation, but to be parents affects more than one. Indeed, the effect of parenthood is tremendous. Now in addressing this topic of parenthood in these two letters Paul mentions only the fathers and not the mothers. This is quite a surprise to me and I do not know for sure why he did so. Certainly, both the father and the mother are responsible for the upbringing of their children. In this regard, Proverbs 1:8 states this: "Hear, my son, the instruction of thy father, and forsake not the teaching of thy mother." Clearly, then, the responsibility of bringing up children rests upon both the father and the mother. The mother is responsible equally with the father in bringing up their children.

As a matter of fact, in the Bible as well as in extra-Biblical history we are shown repeatedly how mothers have greatly influenced their children for good. Take the Israelite prophet Samuel, for instance. I think all of God's people love Samuel, yet they may forget that Samuel had such a good mother, Hannah. It was through her constant prayer and faithfulness that her son ever became Israel's great prophet. Then there is the case of Moses. Although he was brought up by his mother for only a little while—only until he was weaned—nevertheless, she was able to instill God in him in such a way that even after forty years dwelling in Egypt's ruling palace imbibing all the learning and rubbing shoulders with all the luxury and all the corruption of Pharaoh's court none of that unparalleled experience could take God away from that young man. Surely, she was a tremendous mother! Let us also consider Mary, the mother of the Lord Jesus. She had committed herself completely to God, and out of her womb came the Savior of the world. We can likewise cite Paul's young disciple, Timothy, who had such an excellent mother, Eunice, and a very good grandmother, Lois.

Then, too, when we look at the world's history outside that of the Bible, we can read about the mothers of such noteworthy sons as Augustine and John Wesley. Through the unending tears of his mother Monica, Augustine eventually came to the Lord. And with respect to John Wesley, as well as his noteworthy brother Charles, their faithful mother, Susanna Wesley, brought up all her numerous children in the Lord. Throughout Biblical and non-Biblical history there have been many instances of wonderful mothers who exerted immense influence for good upon their children. But strange to say, in both Ephesians and Colossians Paul only mentions the fathers: "Fathers, do not provoke your children to anger. Fathers, do not vex their hearts, that they be not disheartened."

I must acknowledge that I cannot for certain explain why. Are not the mothers responsible for bringing up children? They definitely are. Then why is it that in both these letters of Paul's the emphasis is on the fathers alone? I have wondered, of course, whether it is because many fathers are so occupied with the things of this world—with their jobs, with their social relationships—that they neglect their responsibility towards their children. In many families the fathers simply do not take up their responsibilities as they should. Instead, too often they leave it to the mothers to take care of everything.

Perhaps that is one reason which can explain why. The Holy Spirit most certainly knows how the fathers are likely to end up conducting themselves in this area of responsibility. Therefore, there is singular emphasis placed on just the fathers.

There is probably yet another reason. Usually, it is the father who provokes the children, not the mother. Not a few fathers are too strict and demanding; they thus are *too* responsible! And because of that, they end up vexing their children. Yes, there *are* mothers who, like quite a few fathers, demand of their children quite much, but mothers usually do not do that.

Now I have long wondered whether it is in fact these two reasons which explain why the teaching in the Scriptures on this area of parental responsibility seems to be focused solely on the fathers. Yet we must remember that the mothers are included in this area because they are co-partners with the fathers. So we must safely conclude that in the family not only fathers are responsible for the bringing up of the children but also the mothers, who more often than not help out the fathers greatly in this particular area.

Parents As Stewards

I would like to share some thoughts from God's word concerning the parents first and then some thoughts concerning the children. First of all, parents need to realize that to have children is a tremendous responsibility. God entrusts one or more human beings—each with a spirit and soul and body (cf. I Thessalonians 5:23b)—into the hands of parents. One cannot imagine a trust more serious than that. If a person should trust you with a million dollars, it is only a million dollars. If a person should trust you with a country, it is just a country. But to trust you with a human being—possessing not only a body but also a soul and a spirit—and doing so not only for a time but for eternity: that is indisputably a *tremendous* trust, if we would meditate on the matter if even only for a short while. I am afraid most parents do not realize that in the person of each of their children God is entrusting into their hands a living soul, a personality, a unique life whom He values highly. How that life is going to grow and be developed—whether developed into proper manhood or womanhood or end up being a total failure, disgrace and disaster—is in the parents' hands. Parents therefore need to realize the extraordinary responsibility which God has entrusted to them. In giving children to you it indicates that God considers you to be trustworthy and is thus honoring you. You who are now parents and those who are to be so, do please realize that God honors you to such an extent as to entrust living souls into your hands. What an honor it therefore is to have children! Yet, additionally, what a responsibility to have children!

Furthermore, I would caution you parents not to think that children are solely your property. Yes, in one sense they do belong to you; in quite another sense, however, they do not. Parents must look upon themselves as stewards to whom God has given children in order that the parents may bring them up in the nurture and discipline of the Lord. God has entrusted you with a uniquely important work. In fact, bringing up children properly is the greatest work in the world; it being far more important even than your job.

Depend on the Lord

Hence, because God honors you parents by entrusting precious children into your hands, how very necessary it is for you to be before the Lord for wisdom, guidance, and enabling power. Yet how strange it is that married partners, once they have children, assume they automatically know how—and even have the ability—to be parents. Probably that is why there are such failures. You as parents need to thoroughly understand what God has entrusted you with and how you therefore need to be on your knees looking earnestly to God for mercy, for grace, and for the love needed for such an undertaking! In other words, parents must humbly bow before Him and pray: "Lord, You have honored me with such a trust. I acknowledge that I do not know how to bring up these children for You, nor do I have the power. You have to help me: You must be my wisdom, You need to guide and lead me, You have to teach me how." If you will truly seek

God and look to Him for His grace and mercy, you will find His grace is sufficient for you (cf. II Corinthians 12:9a). But if you should try to be parents all on your own, how easy it will be to end up a failure!

"Do Not Provoke Your Children to Anger"

"Ye fathers, do not provoke your children to anger, but bring them up in the discipline and admonition of the Lord." Too often there are manifested two extremes of parenting. Some parents dare not teach and discipline their children; instead, they let their children run wild. One notion in today's child psychology calls for parents to not hurt their children; rather, they must let them develop their own personality. This modern notion says that if parents try to discipline or teach the children, they will not be able to develop their personalities freely. Therefore, declare modern child psychologists to parents, Lay your hands off and simply let the children grow naturally. Yet for them to grow naturally means wildly!

The other extreme is for some parents to take up their responsibility most seriously—yet they do so not in dependence upon the Lord but upon themselves according to their own wisdom, strength and effort. They discipline and rule over their children with such a heavy hand that their children lose heart.

In contrast to these extremes the word of God is quite balanced. We read: "Fathers, do indeed discipline and admonish your children in the Lord but do not provoke them to anger." Yes, you should teach and discipline your children (and which I will address more fully in a few minutes), but you should also not do certain things which can result in vexing them to the point that they become disheartened. There are especially two things parents do towards their children which contribute to their becoming angry, vexed, and ultimately disheartened.

Parents Show Partiality

If parents are not fair but partial in their dealings with their various children, that alone can provoke the latter to anger. Let me not hear the claim that none of you parents is partial. I recall very well an episode that occurred among my siblings and me. My parents had seven children, but let me be quick to say that this particular episode did not involve my father and mother. We had a lady missionary from the American state of Virginia who lived with us for awhile. (She was the one God used, incidentally, to bring my father to the Lord; and we called her Grandma.) Of the seven children, she loved my youngest brother the best; it was so obvious that he was her favorite. Oftentimes we other children would tease her to get her excited. We would thus say to her: "You are not fair. You are partial. You love our brother more than anybody else." She denied it, saying: "Oh no, I love you all just the same." We persisted: "No, that is not true." She instantly became excited and would try to tell us that she loved us all impartially. Finally, Grandma acknowledged the fact of her favoritism towards our youngest brother by explaining: "The reason is that your brother is closest to me. None of you others comes close to me. That is the reason why." Now in fairness to Grandma, I should add that she may have had a legitimate reason!

Anyway, it seems to be naturally difficult for parents to be equally fair to all the children in their family. Some will appeal to you more than others. Perhaps, for example, they have your personality; so, naturally speaking, it is quite easy for one or the other parent to be partial. When parents manifest partiality towards this or that child, when they are not fair in dealing with all their children in equal fashion, this can provoke anger among the children. They will readily observe that this or that sibling of theirs can get away with doing or saying certain things but they themselves cannot. And why? It is because the parents are showing favoritism; they are not fair and impartial towards all their offspring.

Parents Demand Too Much

There is another and very harmful way parents can provoke their children to anger. Sometimes it is by demanding too much. Some parents will have had an ideal for themselves personally which they had wanted to achieve but had failed to do so. Therefore, they will simply transfer their personal private ideals onto their children. In whatever way they had *failed* they will now want their children to *succeed*. To explain it another way, such parents intend to see that their children live up to their unfulfilled dreams. In so doing, these parents do not respect the personalities of their children; and because of that, they demand and demand and demand. They want their children to achieve that perfect dream of theirs. But when parents do this to their children, they vex them and dishearten them. The children end up feeling they will never be able to attain to that place of perfection. For because the parents are always demanding and never appreciating or praising them, the children finally give up and declare to themselves in frustration and anger: "I am no good. No matter what I do, it is just not good enough. I can never measure up to my parents' expectations. So why should I try anymore?" God's word to the parents is quite clear: Do not vex and anger your children lest they become disheartened. You must therefore respect their personalities and not be forever demanding this and that while at the same time failing to praise and appreciate them or else failing to do so enough.

Admonish and Discipline in the Lord

Now I said a few moments ago that the word of God is so balanced: parents are told, on the one hand, to not provoke their children to anger; and in the next breath they are told to bring them up in the admonition and the discipline of the Lord. It is this latter aspect to God's balanced word that I wish to address next.

Some parents merely take care of and supply the physical needs of their children and let them loose, free of any moral or ethical character training. These parents faithfully do provide food for their children; they also naturally provide a dwelling place for them; they likewise provide clothes for them and finance their schooling and even give them some spare pocket money. But that is the extent of their care and responsibility towards their children. To put it bluntly, these parents are only providing physically for their children's bodies. They have not fulfilled their entire responsibility.

Children's physical well-being is but one of the areas of the parents' responsibility. The parents are to care for not only their children's bodily and physical health but their soulical and spiritual health as well. In other words, parents must teach and admonish their children. Admonishing is probably expressed mostly in words. At times you parents will have to admonish them with words—with teaching. Discipline, on the other hand, is probably expressed mostly by action: sometimes words must be accompanied with action. If there are only words and no action, those words appear vain, and thus they will not be respected. Children ofttimes must be admonished and disciplined together in order to properly bring them up in the Lord.

Now, obviously, God's word does not say that you must admonish and discipline your children according to *yourself*; not so; you are to do so *according to the Lord*. In this connection, Hebrews 12 reminds us that our parents chastise or chasten us according to *their* thought and will. However, this same passage tells us that the heavenly Father chastens us with a *perfect* will in order that we may be partakers of His holiness (v. 10). We should not admonish or discipline our children according to our will; instead, as Christian parents we must admonish and/or discipline them according to the perfect will of God. That is the difference.

As is well known, I come out of a Chinese background, and an old Chinese concept was for children to be considered as the property of the parents. Parents could therefore do whatever they wished to their children, just as they could with any of their physical possessions or property. And the parents were never considered wrong in doing so: they could discipline their children or utter whatever words to them according to their personal whim or wish because their children were deemed to be part of their property. But such a notion is not to be found in the word of God. Rather, there we find that children are God's possession and the parents are simply His stewards who manage those children for Him. For that reason, parents must admonish their children and discipline them according to God's will and not their own.

Today are we as Christian parents admonishing and disciplining our children according to God's teaching? Are we doing so because we want it or because this is what God wants? If only parents would follow what God wills and wants, what a change would occur and what a difference it would make in the way they bring up children. On the one hand, this is a tremendous responsibility resting upon the parents; on the other hand, the responsibility is God's. You parents have Him to depend on and look to—yet not in your way but in His way.

These, then, are but the main principles which the Scriptures teach with regard to the right relationship which parents ought to have with their children.

Practical Measures in Raising Children

I would wish next, however, to bring to our attention some of the practical measures parents must adopt if they are to bring up their children as the Lord desires.

Sanctify Yourselves

In practical terms, the first measure the parents must take is to sanctify themselves for the sake of their children. Let us clearly understand that in the family there cannot be double standards. As grown-ups parents are free to do and say many things and go here and there as they wish, with nothing being wrong or sinful in engaging in these things themselves. But if they then turn around and forbid their children to do the same, this leaves the children perplexed and unable to understand. Yes, perhaps you have a legitimate right to engage in certain activities because you are grown up, but the children will not be able to understand why at their age they are not allowed to do likewise. Consequently, if you as parents do not sanctify yourselves for their sake, you will never be able to teach and discipline them effectively. Consider the Lord Jesus. John 17 tells us that He sanctified himself for our sake (v. 19a). There were many things Jesus could do and say and there would have been nothing wrong in His having done so. Yet for our sake He set himself apart, refraining from doing and saying those things in order that He might not offend us in any way.

Before you ever have children there are probably things which you can do freely, but after you have children you have to think of them. You as a parent will need to consider very seriously and ask yourself: "If I say or do a particular thing or go to a particular place, how will it affect my children? If I tell them not to say this nor do that nor go here or there, but I myself do these things, will this not be establishing a double standard?" Many children rebel against their parents because by their words and actions they create double standards in the family. And as a result parents lose the respect of their children. Not only will they not respect you as a parent anymore; they also will not heed your teaching or receive your discipline—and all because they think you are a hypocrite. Therefore, the first and most practical measure parents must take is to sanctify themselves for the sake of their children. Such will be part of the cross you as parents must take up. For the ongoing well-being of your children in their being willing to receive at your hands the necessary teaching and discipline of the Lord, you voluntarily give up doing or saying certain things that had heretofore been your right in order that you may create and maintain but one standard in the family for all to adhere to. I believe this is very necessary.

Live before God

There is an important second necessary measure parents must adhere to if they are to bring up their children rightly: both father and mother must live before God. There is no way to help the children spiritually if the parents do not live in His presence. If the parents fear God, the children will also fear Him. If the parents love God, the children will love Him as well. You parents must provide the right atmosphere by being the best examples possible for them. The parents will need to live before God if they are ever going to be able to bring their children to Him.

Be of One Mind

Let us consider a third measure: both parents must constantly be of one mind in teaching and disciplining their children. Children are very clever, more clever than we adults may think. Indeed, how well they can play the father against the mother and the mother against the father! The children know that the father will say "no" to certain requests, so they go to the mother. On the other hand, with regard to certain other matters, they know the mother will say "no"; and hence, they will go to the father. By their often successfully playing one parent against another they cause the father and mother various kinds of conflict and disagreement. That is mankind's natural cleverness coming forth. Therefore, in teaching and disciplining the children, the parents have to be of one mind continually. Give them no opportunity, allow no loopholes. If the children should go and speak to the mother, the latter should immediately respond: "What does your father say?" And the same should be done if the children go first to the father. You parents must always be of one mind; otherwise, you will be unable to bring up your children as they should be brought up.

Teach and Discipline in All Areas of Life

A fourth practical measure to be faithfully observed by the parents is this: children are to be taught and disciplined in *all* areas of their lives. Parents should not merely give their children money, or supply them with material needs such as food, clothing and shelter. Though that aspect of life is important, it actually constitutes the smallest part of parenting. Parents must also bring up their children in such other areas of their lives as manners, pathway of life, habits, work, character, relationships, etc. These too need to be taught or to have discipline applied.

For instance, children must be taught *manners*. This has reference not only to table manners but also to manners when they meet others. How should they meet with people? They need to be taught courtesy towards others. Many children today are growing up without receiving any instruction in this life area. Not many manifest good manners anymore because they have not been taught.

Children should also be taught *values*. What things in life are truly valuable? They need to be helped in this area by parents providing them with a standard of values. If, when they are young, children learn what has true value and what has not, they will be kept from making many mistakes. Parents need to teach their children from a very young age what are the things of value in life.

Parents should likewise teach their children *moral standards* when they are young. And these standards need to be faithfully kept. Additionally, children should be taught how to use money wisely and how to give—how to be charitable.

Moreover, you as parents should teach your children how to *work* and how to be diligent in their work. I do thank my parents that when we children were young, all seven of us brothers and sisters had to do some work in our home. Our mother would give each of us a certain task to do, such as sweeping the floor, carrying out the trash, or other similar duties. She assigned to us various responsibilities. Many of today's children do not know how to work. And why? Because they are being served all the time instead. They need to be taught how to work and to serve others.

Thus children are in need of all kinds of training in character-building. Not only do they need to be taught but even disciplined, where necessary, in all these areas of life so that when they arrive at manhood and womanhood, it will be a source of joy and not grief to all concerned. Such, then, is the responsibility of the parents.

Keep Your Promises

Yet a fifth practical measure parents must always observe if their children are to be properly brought up has to do with the parents' words uttered and promises made. Briefly stated, parents' words must always be accurate and their promises must always be kept. Often, parents make a promise to their children and then they simply forget about it. That is quite hurtful to the children. Whatever you as a parent say, it must be accurate and it must be fulfilled. If what you say is not carried out, your words soon become worthless. When you utter something, it has to be accurate and has to be realized. That is the proper way to bring up children in this regard.

Bring Your Children to the Lord

Sixth, and not the least of all, parents have the responsibility of bringing their children to the Lord. That is by far the most essential measure parents must take if their children are to be brought up in the right way. Many parents fail in this responsibility. They do not bring their children to the Lord; instead, they allow them to slip gradually into the world. Then, somebody else—perhaps others in the church—must go out and bring them to the Lord. If the parents would fulfill their responsibility of bringing their children up as God would wish and leading them to the Lord, their children would stay in the church and be useful in the church. Then, the parents and others would not have to go out into the world to rescue them.

These are but a few of the practical measures which I believe parents would find extremely valuable to adopt. There are many, many others, but these few are offered here as a helpful reminder. Oh, how needful it is for parents to raise up their children in the teaching and the discipline of the Lord!

Instructions for Children

I would now like to share some thoughts concerning the children. The word of God has very definite teaching on how to be children according to God's will and desire. This, too, we find in both the Ephesian and Colossian letters. And the teaching or instructions for children given in these two epistles will be our focus.

"Children: Obey Your Parents"

Let us notice, first of all, that the Ephesian and Colossian instructions related to children center exclusively on but one word: obey. Here we read: "Children obey your parents in all things, for this is just"; and also, "Children, obey your parents in all things, for this is well-pleasing to the Lord." Hence, the single, most central instruction given in the Scriptures for children to bear in mind and adhere to is to obey their parents.

Let us all—both adults and children—realize that the Bible uses words very carefully. For example, with respect to the wives in their relationship to their husbands, the word employed is *submit*. But with respect to the children as to how they are expected to relate to their parents, it is *obey*. Now why is this? It is because submission is an inward attitude. As we saw earlier, according to the Scriptures the husband and the wife are "fellow-heirs of the grace of life" (I Peter 3:7b). In other words, the husband and the wife—as partners in marriage—are equal; therefore, the word employed in the Bible for characterizing the relationship of wife to husband is submit. It is an inward attitude expressing itself in the form of submission. On the other hand, parents and children are not equal. Today, many children think they are equal with their parents, or even superior to them. But the Bible tells us that the parents and the children are not equal. The parents occupy a position which is on a higher level. Therefore, the relationship of the children to their parents is one of obedience.

To obey is an outward action. Oftentimes children may not understand why their parents want them to *do* certain things or why they do *not* want them to do those things. If in their immaturity children need to understand everything their parents have instructed them to do in order for them to obey, they will not be able to. Nevertheless, many children will still ask, "Well, why?"—as though if they do not see a good reason to do or not do something, they will not obey. They are just not able to know why or to understand fully because they are not mature enough yet. And yet obedience is not a matter of understanding. In contrast to submission which is an inward attitude, obedience, by its very nature, is expressed in outward acts. Whether children understand or not, they must nonetheless obey.

Now obviously if a child can understand why, it is better. It is true, of course, that if your parents are willing to explain the matter to you, that can be most helpful. But when it comes to obedience, whether you as a child or youngster understand or not, it is incumbent upon you to obey because, as Ephesians tells us, that is just. Where is to be seen the justice in this? The justice lies in the fact that your parents are quite extensively taking care of you. Are they not continually providing you with many of life's necessities? Do they not have the responsibility of bringing you up? And, thus, having such a responsibility over you, it is but just for you to obey them. If you receive so much from your parents, and yet you refuse to obey them, *you* are being *un*just. It is therefore just for children to obey their parents.

Well, sometimes you children may say that your parents do not know as much as you do. That may very well be true in certain areas. But you cannot disobey simply because they may not know more than you do. Consider the boy Jesus and the event recorded in Luke 2 about Him. When He was twelve, He was made a son of the law in the temple. And now realizing in that capacity His responsibility towards His Father, He remained behind in the temple when His earthly parents were returning home to Nazareth from their yearly journey to Jerusalem for the Passover Feast. Upon going back to Jerusalem and after searching three days for Him, they finally found Him still in the temple. His mother Mary inquired of Him: "Son, why have You treated us like this? Why did You not return home with us? See how anxious we have been about You"

(vv. 46-48). The Lord Jesus replied: "Did you not know and understand that I must be in My Father's house and occupied with My Father's business?" By this time Jesus had realized that He was God's Son and that He must therefore be about His Father's business. And yet, His parents did not know or understand any of this (v. 50). Did the boy Jesus now refuse in disobedience to go back home with His parents because they did not know or understand? The Bible narrative clearly tells us that He did return home with His parents and *obeyed* them (v. 51a). There in continual obedience Jesus grew in grace and in the favor of God His Father (v. 52).

Hence, let me say to the children that even if you think you are superior to your parents, considering them to be antiques and that you know better, nevertheless, it is your duty to obey. In fact, on some occasions, to obey may mean a cross for you to bear; for the Lord Jesus had told His disciples: "Deny yourself, take up your cross, and follow Me" (see Matthew 10:38, Mark 8:34, Luke 9:23). Indeed, Colossians tells us that children's obedience "in *all* things" is "well-pleasing" to the Lord. Not only is it just, it is also well-pleasing to Him.

Let me ask both teenagers and children: Do you want to please the Lord? It is my firm belief that there is nothing you can do to please Him more than for you to obey your parents.

Trust the Lord

Permit me to continue addressing both teenagers and youngsters by saying the following. If you desire to be the best children possible, then you need, first of all, to trust the Lord; that is to say, you need to believe on Jesus as Savior. Then once you belong to Him, you can be well-pleasing to Him. So, first, trust in the Lord Jesus, asking Him to come into your heart. Accept Him as your personal Savior, learn to love Him and trust Him. If first you put your trust in the Lord, and then as you look to Him, He will enable you to obey your parents in all matters.

Do we adults think children today really rebel against authority? Outwardly, yes, but inwardly, no. Outwardly speaking, it would appear as though children today do rebel against any kind of authority. Yet inwardly, they actually respect authority. And why? They realize that in authority there is security and there is love. When parents do not discipline their children, the latter do not respect them and even think their parents do not love them. Without necessary instruction and discipline children do not have a sense of security. But those who are disciplined in the Lord by their parents know their parents love them enough to discipline them and there is thus a feeling of security for them. Under authority, they are protected. So the Bible teaches children to obey their parents in all things. Children must not argue with them. It is only a very rare case, if any, in which one's parents would demand their children do something that is against the law and will of God. Obviously, in that rare case, children must obey God rather than man. Therefore, other than in such a rare exception, the Bible's unwavering instruction to children is: "Obey your parents in all things, for this is well-pleasing [to] the Lord."

Honor Both Father and Mother

We know that the Law or Ten Commandments were inscribed by the finger of God on two tablets of stone (see, e.g., Exodus 32:15-16, 19; Deuteronomy 5:22, 9:10-11, 10:1-5). The first four of these Ten concern mankind's relationship with God; the last six have to do with mankind's relationship with his fellow man (Exodus 20:1-17, Deuteronomy 5:1-21). Now among these six commandments governing all human relationships the very first one is: "Honour thy father and thy mother." And Ephesians notes that this is a commandment—in fact, the only one of the Ten—with promise; namely, that a person who observes this commandment shall fare well in this life and live very long while on the earth.

How can those of us who are children honor our father and mother? Among all the ways by which to honor them the best one by far is to obey them. Another way to honor them is to listen to them. A third way is to seek their advice. Yet another way is to accept their discipline. And still another way to honor them is to communicate with them and learn from them. These are some of the ways to honor our parents.

Many children today do not communicate with their parents. They seek advice from outside but not from them. Indeed, they do not listen to their parents and even despise them. Such are not the ways of honoring one's parents. To show honor is to draw near to them and communicate with them, pour out one's heart to them, seek their advice and heed it, accept their discipline, and, above all, obey them. Such is the way children can honor their father and mother. And God has promised that in so doing children shall live well and live long on the earth.

Let me add by way of conclusion that if in all our families both parents and children together learn to be in the Lord and for the Lord, if they all learn to look to God and learn to live by the life of Christ in them, then we shall witness God's blessing upon our families. Moreover, those same families shall most certainly bear a winsome testimony to the world. All this God is able to bring about if both parents and children faithfully live according to the instructions given in His word. May we all bring glory to His name.

Our heavenly Father, how we praise and thank Thee that Thou dost desire to have families that would be a glory to Thy name. Oh, how we praise and thank Thee that Thou dost not only tell us what

Thou dost expect of the parents and of the children but that Thou dost also give us Thy life and with that source of power we can be parents and can be children according to Thy will. So, Father, we ask Thee that we all—as either parents or children—may humble ourselves before Thee and trust Thee and look to Thy light so that we all may be a glory to Thy name. We ask in the name of our Lord Jesus. Amen.

Chapter Seven
Serving God with the Family

Joshua 24:15b—As for me and my house, we will serve Jehovah.

We have been fellowshiping together on this vital subject of the family and God's purpose for it. First of all, we came to realize that *God* originated the family, not man. It is a divine concept, not just a human idea. God created man as a family, male and female created He them, and He brought them together to be one. It was to this family that God commanded: "Be fruitful and multiply, and fill the earth, and subdue it."

Before sin came into this world the first family on earth had been an ideal family. Not only did the man and the woman love each other, they also were under God who came down and fellowshiped with them. Moreover, these two were one. Unfortunately, however, sin entered the world and destroyed this ideal family life. But thank God, in the redemption of His Son Jesus, He once more held the family in view: "Believe on the Lord Jesus and thou shalt be saved, *and thy house*."

Now in order to establish a family which is according to God's thought, redeemed mankind must first begin by choosing to have the right mate: Christians, we are instructed in God's word, are not to be unequally yoked with unbelievers. It is His will that only two believers—a redeemed man and a redeemed woman—should be joined into one as husband and wife, and only then will that family be on the right footing as God would have it.

We are then instructed in God's word how to be husbands and how to be wives. God instructs the husbands to love their wives as Christ loved the church and gave himself up for her. He also instructs the wives to submit to their husbands as to the Lord himself. If both will live in and by the life of Christ, then the husband will know how and be empowered to be the head of the family and the wife will know how and be empowered to be its body. In thus working together, that family will be rightly established in God's sight.

Then, in God blessing that family with children, He next instructs in His word how to be parents and how to be children in the relationship between these two components of the family. As we saw last time, children are to obey their parents in all things, for this is just and is well-pleasing to the Lord; and fathers are not to provoke their children to anger lest they become disheartened and are to bring them up in the admonition and the discipline of the Lord.

If all the above divine instructions are fully put into practice, we shall witness a family that is truly under God. Indeed, in that family Christ is the acknowledged Head and the husband himself represents Christ as its head; the wife serves as the body that supports the family; the children obey their parents; and the parents bring up the children in the admonition and discipline of the Lord. Can a family be more beautiful than that? With such a family as this, God will be highly honored!

God's Purpose for the Family

What, though, is God's purpose for the family? Too many of us think that the only purpose for having a family is that we may enjoy ourselves, that we may find satisfaction in life. Now, of course, in giving men and women families God does desire us to enjoy ourselves and one another and to find satisfaction in family life. Yet that is not God's primary purpose for having families. If that were the case, we would all be living at a very low and selfish level. No, the primary purpose in God's thought for having families is that we may serve Him with our families. If a family does not serve God, that family has nullified its primary meaning and purpose.

The Background to Joshua's Public Declaration

Let us look at the life of Joshua—one of the Old Testament period's preeminent servants of God—in considering the background to his remarkable public declaration: "As for me and my house, we will serve the Lord." Joshua issued this public statement when he was well-advanced in age. When he was a young man, he was chosen by Moses to lead the children of Israel in their fight against the Amalekites (Exodus 17:8-10a). God's people had never fought a battle before, so this was their first experience in warfare. The children of Israel had come out of Egypt into the wilderness desert, and while there the Amalekites had attacked them from the rear at the moment when the Israelites were very weary and some of them had lingered behind (Deuteronomy 25:17-18).

Having been chosen by Moses to lead the people in battle, Joshua gathered the Israelites together and went forth in battle against the Amalekites. And we will recall that Moses went atop a nearby hill to intercede before God on behalf of the Israelites; and as long as his hands remained lifted up in intercessory prayer, Joshua was able to overcome the enemy until he completely defeated them (17:10b-13). This is the first mention of Joshua in the Bible—a young man who successfully fought against the Amalekites.

Now in the Scriptures the Amalekites serve as a type or symbol of the flesh. The flesh in our human make-up is like the Amalekites. Its wrong influence always comes upon us when we are weak. But here was a young man who overcame, as it were, the flesh as represented by these attacking Amalekites. For a young man to overcome his flesh is quite a remarkable achievement. Many, if not most, young people today readily give in to the lusts and the desires of their flesh. But here was a young man who had strictly dealt with his flesh by disciplining himself and was able to overcome by the grace of God. Through prayer—the prayer of Moses—Joshua overcame that which represented the flesh—the Amalekites.

Moses subsequently chose this young man to be his assistant (Exodus 24:13). And when Moses ascended Mount Sinai to receive the Ten Commandments, Joshua went up with him (again, Exodus 24:13). It is true that Moses left Joshua behind at the mid-point of his ascent to the summit and went on alone to the top of the mountain; nevertheless, Joshua remained on the mountain during the entire time his master did. In fact, Moses waited before God at the summit for forty days and forty nights (Exodus 24:18). We too often forget about Joshua in this episode. We assume that it was only Moses who was forty days and forty nights on the mountain waiting upon God to receive from Him the Ten Commandments. But there was also on the mount the young man Joshua for those many days and nights. He was near Moses during the entire period, after which he accompanied Moses when Moses came down and saw the golden calf by which the Israelites, having worshiped and offered sacrifices to it, had sinned against God (Exodus 32:7-8, 15-19a). Breaking the Tablets of the Law into pieces, Moses henceforth had the Tent of the Lord's Presence or the Tent of Meeting (the precursor to the Tabernacle) set up some distance away outside the Israelites' camp (Exodus 25:8, 33:7-11b). And the Bible narrative tells us that "Joshua ... departed not from within the tent" of meeting (33:11c). What an extraordinary young man he was!

In all this we see that Joshua was a young man who continually was very near to God—not only on the Sinai Mount for that lengthy period but also we read that he "remained" at the Tent of Meeting. Joshua had rich fellowship and communion with God. It was no wonder that he had the strength to overcome the flesh.

We next learn from the Scriptures that when God's people arrived at the border of the Promised Land, Joshua and Caleb were two of the twelve spies who were sent to spy out the land. Now when these two came back, they reported to the people in a most positive way and encouraged them, saying: "We will go in and possess the land as God has promised because He is with us. Indeed, these inhabitants of the land, though they be giants, shall be our food." By contrast, the ten other spies were frightened and brought only evil reports. Only Joshua—along with Caleb—had an excellent spirit (Numbers 13:25-33, 14:6-10, 24, 30-31, 36-38). Here, then, was a young man whose whole heart was set upon Jehovah God. Joshua had a beautiful spirit and whose heart to serve Him alone never wavered from serving God.

Furthermore, before Moses died Joshua was chosen to be his successor (Numbers 27:15-19, 23). In fact, it was under Joshua that the children of Israel entered the Promised Land (Deuteronomy 31:1-3, 7-8). As an encouragement the word of God came to Joshua, saying:

"Be strong and courageous. Do not be afraid. As I was with Moses, I will be with you. No one shall be able to stand before you. Keep the commandments. Meditate upon My word day and night" (see Deuteronomy 31:14-15, 23; Joshua 1:1, 5-9). Thus, it was in the strength of the Lord that Joshua brought the children of Israel into the Promised Land. He conquered the enemies therein and apportioned the land among Israel's twelve tribes.

Such, then, was the background to this man's stirring late-in-life public announcement. For now being well-advanced in age, this servant of God, in his last service to the children of Israel, gathered all the nation's leaders, judges, officers, elders and all the children of Israel to the town of Shechem. There he presented them all to God, declaring as he did so these words: "God has done so much for you; nevertheless, you are free to choose whether you wish to serve Him or you wish to serve other gods; it is up to you. But whatever may be *your* choice, *my* choice has long before this moment been made: As for me and my house, we will [continue to] serve the Lord" (see Joshua 24:1-2, 15).

When he was a young man, Joshua had served God with all his heart. Then he married and had a family, and he set a good example, living an exemplary life in the family as a good husband and father, and leading his whole family in serving the Lord. So that in his public statement and declaration to the children of Israel, "As for me and my house," Joshua not only referenced himself—

"me"—but also included his entire family—"my house"—that is to say, "My wife, my children, and I," declared Joshua, "all in my family serve the Lord. No matter what your choice may be, we serve the Lord."

Entire Family Is to Serve God

What a beautiful testimony that is! This, then, is God's purpose in our having a family: He gives us families and raises up families that we, as families and not as individual family members, may serve Him. It is not to be just one member in the family serving God, nor is it to be just the father and the mother serving Him, nor is it to be just the children serving Him. In many instances, unfortunately, there is but one member in a given family serving God; the rest are not serving Him. These other members may all be saved, yet they are not serving God; or, they may not be saved at all. Sometimes we see the parents, both husband and wife, serving God, but the children do not follow their example and serve. On the other hand, we may find in other families that the young people truly love God and serve Him, but their parents do not. However, God's will is that the whole family should serve Him. All of us in our families should serve God—both old and young, men and women, parents and children, husband and wife. The entire family should rise up and make service towards God the fundamental meaning and purpose for their family.

Allow me to inquire, What is the purpose of *your* family? You may have a purpose for yourself individually, but is there a purpose for your family? Have you realized that God has given you a family for a divine reason? It is for you and your family to serve God together. It is only through the service of the family that God's purpose on this earth can be fulfilled.

Let me put this matter to you in the following way. In the opening pages of God's word we read that after He created man as a family, He then blessed that family and said, "Be fruitful and multiply, and fill the earth, and subdue it." In spiritual terms, God was here entrusting that family with a tremendous mission. His intention was to use that family to defeat His enemy, restore the earth, bring in His kingdom, and bring in His glory. It was all to be done through that family. We all know, of course, that that first family failed. At the end of God's word, however, we again find a family. There, we learn that through *that* family the enemy, in prophetic fulfillment, is defeated, the kingdom of God is brought in, and God is glorified.

Now who or what is that family? That is the family of God, the church. In other words, at the inception of all things, we see merely the very first family whom God has created and to whom he has entrusted His great mission. Then, over the long span of human history, God's Son ultimately gains for himself a huge family, the family or church of God. And it is through that family that God's purpose is finally fulfilled. But let us realize that the church of God—indeed, the immense family of God—is made up of uncountable Christian families; and that therefore, every family in the family of God has been entrusted with a tremendous work: to serve God and to serve His purpose for the family.

A Family That Served God

Now how do we serve God and His purpose as a family? There is provided for us in the Bible a beautiful picture of a family that served God together as one (Luke 10:38-42). From the human standpoint it was not a family that was very sufficient or at all prominent—at least not until Jesus entered the picture. This was the family of Martha, Mary and Lazarus. It was a small family residing in a small village called Bethany. It was a family which had almost nothing. Moreover, the Bible narrative does not mention either the father or the mother; so very likely they both had died early and had left behind them two daughters and one son as orphans. From the human standpoint, therefore, how could such an inadequate, insufficient, poor and destitute family serve God? And yet this family did.

Many of us might be of the opinion that if a family desires to serve God, it needs to have and be that which would recommend itself for serving the almighty God. Not so. True, here was a poor, obscure family that was without parents, consisting of but two sisters and a brother, that dwelt in a tiny village and that had no means for residing nearby in Jerusalem, the capital, less than two miles away. And yet, this was a family home to which the Lord Jesus would return again and again during His earthly lifetime. For the Bible tells us that even during His last week on earth, when daily He would travel the short distance over to Jerusalem in His final effort to reach His people with the gospel concerning himself, Jesus would leave Jerusalem every evening and return to this home at Bethany (John 12:1, 12, with all the ff.: John 11:18; Mark 11:1, 11, 12a, 19; Matthew 21:1, 17; Luke 19:28, 47a; 21:37-38). Without any doubt, it was a household He loved to visit; in fact, He loved to go there and live. Why was this? It was because this brother and two sisters served Him not just as individuals but as a family.

We are told in Luke's Gospel, chapter 10, that when Jesus went to that village He was received and welcomed by this particular little family. There surely were other families in Bethany which were more complete and richer by far, but the Lord did not go to any of them. Instead, He went to this poor, obscure family because, as Luke 10 tells us, Martha opened their home to Him (v. 38). How apt is the statement in chapter 1 of John's Gospel: Jesus came to His own and His own received Him not; but as many as received Him, who believed in His name, to them He gave the right to become children of God (v. 12). The world for the most part rejected the Lord Jesus; and yet, here was a little family whose members all received Him with whole hearts. It is easily understandable, therefore, that it was to this family that Jesus would always go when in Bethany. In a sense, the Lord had found His home in that family.

Two Sides to Serving the Lord

Now on this first occasion of Jesus entering the home of Mary, Martha and Lazarus, this, we will recall, is what happened: Martha had busied herself with preparing and serving food for the Lord. And though, unlike in a rich household, the food might be meager, it was being prepared by Martha with a full heart. For she was very busy preparing the meal as best she could. Indeed, she was much busier than usual because she wanted to provide something special for Jesus. And hence, Martha had become distracted by these extra preparations; so much so that she did not know what to do: she had grown nervous and tense because of her sincere desire to do the very best she could for the Lord. So we ought not blame Martha. Some people might assume that Jesus actually scolded Martha because she was preparing a meal for Him and not doing what her sister Mary was doing. Not so. Martha had wanted to serve the Lord in the best way possible. Here, then, is the scene before us of Martha busily occupied in preparing this special meal while her sister Mary was seated at Jesus' feet intently listening to His every word (vv. 39-40a).

Let us pause and consider what serving the Lord actually is. Does it not include both these activities? On the one hand, serving the Lord is to be engaged in doing things for Him. Serving the Lord does not mean we have become so spiritual that we are no longer practical. No, serving Him has its practical side. We ought to be engaged in doing things so that the Lord may receive something from us, and we ought to do them in the best way we can because it is for Him. On the other hand, serving the Lord also means that we sit at His feet and hear Him. Often, God's people are very much engaged in doing things for the Lord but they neglect having fellowship with Him in His word. Let us be clear that it is not that these things should not be done for the Lord and we let Him go hungry. No, these practical undertakings *should* be done, but the problem with many of us is that we forget to sit at the Lord's feet and hear Him. How can we serve Him in practical ways if we do not hear Him first? Consequently, serving the Lord must include these two sides.

Service must *begin* with hearing. That is why, when the Levitical priests were consecrated in the olden days, blood would be put upon their right ear *first* and only then upon the thumb of the right hand and upon the toe of the right foot. In other words, in our serving the Lord the first action is to sit at His feet and hear Him so that we might know His will. We need to wait upon Him to know what His will is for us to do practically, and then we rise up and do it using our hands and feet. Accordingly, these are the two necessary sides in serving the Lord, as represented by Mary and Martha.

The Lord As Head of the Family

Now let us notice that Martha, having become distracted, nervous and tense from her extra meal preparations, went to Jesus and said, "Lord, do You not care that my sister has left me to do all this work and does not help me?" From this action we can discern the fact that the members of this family not only had received the Lord with open hearts but they also, upon His entering their home, had immediately acknowledged that He was the Master and Head of their household. For take note of the fact that Martha did not go to Mary and say, "Please, Mary, come and help me"; she instead went to Jesus and said, "Lord, You are the Head of our family. And You see how busy I am. Will You therefore please tell my sister to come and help me?" Martha automatically recognized Jesus as the Lord and Head of their family (see v. 40b). That, too, is an expression of serving the Lord. And even though Jesus, in His response to Martha (vv. 41-42a), saying, "Martha, you are troubled with many things, yet there is one thing needed and your sister has chosen what is that better portion," nevertheless, the Lord did not scold Martha nor did He reject her service. He only told her not to be tense, nervous and distracted in her service to Him.

Let me ask, Is Jesus the Lord of your family? Is He the Head of your household? If so, then whatever you do as a family, you will inquire of Him; and whatever His will may be, that is what shall be done. We as a family will ask the Head what He wants us to do, for it is all under His direction. If the Lord Jesus is truly the Head of our family, we will not do things as we like; rather, when there is a need, we will go to the Lord Jesus as Head and ask Him how that need should be met, and once we know, we will do so accordingly. Now such a family as that is one which truly serves God.

We will recall that in John 11 we are told that Jesus loved Martha, Mary and Lazarus (v. 5). There was such a warm and deep friendship between the Lord Jesus and these three family members. Every member of that family loved Him and He loved every member. In fact, the greatest miracle Jesus ever performed while on earth was performed within the context of this very family: He raised up Lazarus from the dead (vv. 38-44). Indeed, the greatest truth Jesus ever revealed to mankind was unveiled to this same family: He revealed himself as the Resurrection and the Life (vv. 23-25a). All this is evidence of the great love and deep friendship which marked the relationship between the Lord Jesus and those three family members.

If each of our families will acknowledge Jesus as Head and will love Him as one family, He will manifest himself to each and every family. The Lord will be able to do many wondrous things in our families. He will be able to teach and guide us and reveal great truths to us.

A Feast Held in Jesus' Honor

Now it so happened that a short time after Lazarus had been raised, there was a dinner feast given in Jesus' honor when He once again came to Bethany (John 12:1-11). We do not know if this feast was held in the little home where Martha, Mary and Lazarus lived; probably it occurred in a larger house, for we are told in the Scriptures that a large crowd of Jews came there upon hearing that Jesus was in the town (vv. 1-2, 9). In any case, Jesus was being entertained by His hosts with a lavish dinner held in His honor. And Lazarus and his two sisters were also present along with others who were reclining at the table with the Lord. By carefully observing what this little Bethany family of three members did while attending this feast, we shall come to see three different ways by which we in our own families today can likewise serve the Lord.

Serving the Lord Practically

We shall first notice Martha, who, as usual, was busy serving the food (v. 2). She was there working with her hands in serving the Lord. Once again I would stress that this is an essential side to serving the Lord. Let us not be so spiritual as to assume that service to the Lord is exclusively a matter of our minds. We must use our hands as well if we wish to serve Him completely. Here was Martha serving Jesus in a most practical way. She was most likely involved in helping to prepare, cook, and then serve the food as Jesus and the others were reclining at the dinner table.

Let us therefore apply to ourselves today this aspect of service to the Lord. When, for example, a wife is preparing and serving up food for her family's mealtime enjoyment, she could mentally approach this task by either deeming it as simply being one of many services performed for her family or considering it as also a service to the Lord. It will all depend on that wife's heart attitude. Two different family wives may be engaged in the same family responsibility, but if they view that responsibility in the two opposite ways just described, the result will be like the difference which exists between earth and heaven. It all depends on one's heart attitude.

What is it which is necessary for the wife to recognize that whatever she does in serving her family is likewise serving the Lord? She will need to take her proper place in the family as its body in support of her husband as head, to submit herself to her husband as to the Lord himself, and to have a heart of love towards the Lord. Then the wife can see and realize that all her service for the family is in reality also service to the Lord. Jesus once declared: "Inasmuch as you have done a good deed to the least of My brethren, you have done it to Me" (see Matthew 25:40). Whenever a wife and mother performs for her husband and children the countless tasks which are her responsibilities, she is not only satisfying the members of her family but also satisfying the Lord. Such is the proper understanding of what it means to serve God.

What has just now been said regarding the wife and mother in the family ought to be the same concerning the husband and the children. As the husband is constrained by the love of Christ (cf. II Corinthians 5:14-15) to learn to be the head of the family, provide financially for the family, and bring up the family in the fear and love of the Lord, he too is serving God. And with respect to the children, as they obey their parents in all things, they are serving God as well. Let us not imagine that serving God requires us to undertake some spectacular work. Some, perhaps many, believers are still of the opinion that if they do not go forth as a missionary to the most distant place on the foreign field, they are not serving God. Not true. The Christian can serve God right in his or her home. As all members of the family love the Lord and as they take their respective places in the family and do the will of God, it shall be that no matter what task or good deed their hands take up to perform, such shall be viewed by God as serving the Lord just like Martha. Oh, we really need to serve God in every practical way.

Serving the Lord in Worship

Martha, as was pointed out earlier, represents the practical side to serving the Lord: *doing* things for Him. But there is another aspect to serving, and that is reflected in what Mary chose to do during Jesus' latest visit among this Bethany household. Evidently Mary and Martha were different temperamentally, and, accordingly, God gives to each of His children a different gift or talent. Mary was not skillful in cooking; nevertheless, there was a way for her, too, to serve the Lord. What was Mary moved to do? She came to Jesus holding in her hands an expensive alabaster flask containing a pound of pure nard or perfume. Judas (he the clever economist among the twelve) quickly calculated that this pound of perfume-like ointment was worth three hundred denarii. Back in those days one denarius coin was the actual wage of a man for an entire day's labor; and at that time the women were paid even less. Thus Mary's pound of nard was worth the equivalent of a man's wages for three hundred days (vv. 4-5). For her to have accumulated that amount of money was remarkable. It probably represented her total life's savings. Naturally, being a woman, Mary would want to have some fragrant perfume on hand. Perhaps she was setting it aside for her wedding on some future day. However, she was now so constrained by the love of Christ (see again II Corinthians 5:14-15) that she took that expensive flask of nard, broke it, and poured its entire contents upon Jesus' feet and then used her hair to wipe His feet. Instantly the fragrance spread throughout the house; and thus in this way Mary served the Lord (v.3). How so?

Well, whereas Martha served the Lord by preparing and serving dinner, Mary did so by pouring out her love upon Him. All which she had she poured upon the Lord without reservation because she saw the incomparable worth of the Lord Jesus. Permit me to inquire: How much is the Lord Jesus worth to you? Is He worth a pound of costly pure nard? Judas thought differently: "No, no, He is not worth that. To have done this was a complete waste" (see vv. 4-6). To Mary, however, Jesus was worth even more than her precious pound of ointment, but that was all she had. Now that is worship.

How much is Jesus worth in our eyes? The more we see the worthiness of the Lord, the more we are able to pour out from our heart of love and the more He is worshiped. That, too, is serving the Lord. And such constitutes yet another aspect to serving God.

Serving the Lord As a Witness

We have observed what both sisters in this little family at Bethany did in serving the Lord Jesus during the special feast held in His honor. We shall now learn in what way their brother Lazarus also served the Lord.

Lazarus was among those sitting with Jesus at table enjoying the feast (v. 2). Yet was he simply there enjoying himself as he sat by the Lord? To the contrary, he was there with Him serving as a witness. However, at this moment, for Lazarus to be serving as a witness to the Lord by his resurrected life was a perilous and potentially very costly thing to do. Why so? It was because the Jewish chief priests, who, along with the Pharisees, had already plotted to take Jesus' life, had now made plans to kill Lazarus as well, since many of the people had come to see him who had been raised from the dead and were siding with Jesus and even believing in Him (vv. 9-11).

Interestingly, we are told by tradition that after Lazarus had been raised from the dead, he never once opened his mouth about it. Whether such report is true or not, we do not know. On the one hand, many of us would think that a person who has been resurrected from the grave would be speaking all the time; he would have much to tell, right? Oh, his mouth would never be shut! On the other hand, tradition tells us that Lazarus never spoke of his extraordinary experience, as though it were too sacred an event in his life for him ever to utter a single word. Nevertheless, if tradition be true, then by Lazarus simply reclining with the Lord at dinner, what a witness and testimony his life must have been! For what we do know for certain is that many of the Jews came to see Lazarus and were putting their faith in Jesus. And as a consequence of Lazarus' witness, Jewish leaders had decided that they must do away with him, too.

When all is said and done, how do we in essence serve the Lord? Do we not serve Him by living a life with Him? As we live a life close to the Lord Jesus, the world will see and believe in Him. But it may be costly, it may even cost us our very life. Are we serving the Lord in that respect? In this little family of three, Martha served in one way, Mary in another, and Lazarus in still another. When all three are put together, we see manifested the full service of a family towards the Lord.

Service Extended to God's Family—the Church

Now in applying to ourselves in our own day what has been said about these three family members and their ways of service to Jesus, let us realize and acknowledge that in our serving the Lord we each of us ought at times be Martha, ought at times be Mary, and at times be Lazarus. In other words, all three ways in serving the Lord should together be manifested in and through each one of us. Beyond this, however, God also gives special, different gifts to His people. And hence, we all have an obligation to serve God with the gift and grace He has given to each (Romans 12:6).

Moreover, if we all serve well in our families, then our service will be extended to the larger family of God—the church. In fact, there is a definite relationship between service in the family and service in the church. We find this illustrated by Paul in his I Timothy letter. For example, a man who governs his household well is eligible to be considered as an elder in the church (3:4-5). On the other hand, if a man does not govern his family well, he will not be able to govern that larger family—the church and household of God. Whether positive or negative, there is a relationship there between one's service in the family and one's service in the church.

How praiseworthy it is that God has placed us as members within a family: husband, wife, parents, children. This is God's creative handiwork. As members of our families, all of us should learn to love and serve God in whatever position or capacity each of us occupies which He has given to us. And if everyone learns to serve Him in his or her family, such service will be extended into the church, so that when all families assemble together as the family of God, much service will be present. Especially will there be the practical work and service of Martha. Indeed, many brothers and sisters in the Lord will make themselves available to serve in the church—the family of God—in such practical forms of service as the following: setting up chairs, welcoming people, helping the poor, visiting the sick, showing hospitality to both strangers and saints, etc. The way of practical service all begins in our families but then extends to the larger family of God—the church.

Yet, not only the practical service of Martha has its beginning in our personal families; Mary's service of worship also begins there; and, like the practical side of service, such worthy worship in our families extends to the church as well. For when our families assemble together as the family of God, we together can offer up our appreciation of the Lord in our worship of Him.

What, too, can be said about the kind of service to the Lord rendered by Lazarus? Does not living our life with the Lord likewise have its beginning in us as members of our families? If we, as did Lazarus, live a life close to the Lord there, we shall mutually be serving as witnesses to our fellow family members. And such service to Him as this must surely extend to the church; for when our families come together as the family of God, there will be much which we can share with our brethren out of our experience of being with the Lord in fellowship.

By all these various forms of service the church—as the big family of God—will be established and built up as a testimony to the world.

Family Altar

Finally, let me observe that in order to help strengthen the life of one's family for service, I believe it is important for that family to have a family altar. By this I do not mean that a family has a literal, physical altar. No, that would be an Old Testament understanding. What I mean to be understood as saying is that a family should set aside a time each day for all members to come together to read God's word, to pray, and to worship the

Lord. A few explanations may be necessary according to the understanding of the children; nevertheless, the whole family should be brought together before God at least once every day. Then as the children grow up, He is no longer a stranger to them; instead, they will have become quite familiar with Him. By means of a daily family-altar experience an atmosphere of the love of God will have been created and sustained in the family. If every family will have such a daily experience, and if the family shall truly be together in serving God, the life of His bigger family—the church—will be greatly strengthened.

> *Our heavenly Father, we do praise and thank Thee that Thou dost raise up families to serve Thee. Lord, we would like to declare by faith through Thy grace that as for us and our households, we will serve* Thee. *Oh God, make this a reality. Teach us how to serve Thee in our families and how also to serve Thee together in the church and family of God. Oh God, we do pray that through Thy church, Thy kingdom shall be brought in and Thou shalt be glorified. We ask in the name of our Lord Jesus. Amen.*

OTHER TITLES AVAILABLE
From Christian Fellowship Publishers

By Watchman Nee

<u>The Basic Lesson Series</u>
Vol. 1 - A Living Sacrifice
Vol. 2 - The Good Confession
Vol. 3 - Assembling Together
Vol. 4 - Not I, But Christ
Vol. 5 - Do All to the Glory of God
Vol. 6 - Love One Another

Aids to "Revelation"
Amazing Grace
Back to the Cross
A Balanced Christian Life
The Better Covenant
The Body of Christ: A Reality
The Character of God's Workman
Christ the Sum of All Spiritual Things
The Church and the Work – 3 Vols
"Come, Lord Jesus"
The Communion of the Holy Spirit
The Finest of the Wheat – Vol. 1
The Finest of the Wheat – Vol. 2
From Faith to Faith
From Glory to Glory
Full of Grace and Truth – Vol. 1
Full of Grace and Truth – Vol. 2
Gleanings in the Fields of Boaz
The Glory of His Life
God's Plan and the Overcomers
God's Work
Gospel Dialogue
Grace for Grace
Heart-to-Heart Talks
Interpreting Matthew
Journeying towards the Spiritual
The King and the Kingdom of Heaven
The Latent Power of the Soul
Let Us Pray
The Life That Wins
The Lord My Portion
The Messenger of the Cross
The Ministry of God's Word
My Spiritual Journey
The Mystery of Creation
Powerful According to God
Practical Issues of This Life
The Prayer Ministry of the Church
The Release of the Spirit
Revive Thy Work
The Salvation of the Soul
The Secret of Christian Living
Serve in Spirit
The Spirit of Judgment
The Spirit of the Gospel
The Spirit of Wisdom and Revelation
Spiritual Authority
Spiritual Discernment
Spiritual Exercise
Spiritual Knowledge
The Spiritual Man
Spiritual Reality or Obsession
Take Heed
The Testimony of God
Whom Shall I Send?
The Word of the Cross
Worship God
Ye Search the Scriptures

ORDER FROM: 11515 Allecingie Parkway Richmond, VA 23235
www.c-f-p.com

OTHER TITLES AVAILABLE
From Christian Fellowship Publishers

By Stephen Kaung

The "God Has Spoken" Series
Seeing Christ in the Old Testament, Part One
Seeing Christ in the Old Testament, Part Two
Seeing Christ in the New Testament

Discipled to Christ
The Gymnasium of Christ
In the Footsteps of Christ
New Covenant Living & Ministry
The Songs of Degrees – *Meditations on Fifteen Psalms*
The Splendor of His Ways – *Seeing the Lord's End in Job*